Arquitectura-G

Director and Editor of *2G* Moisés Puente
Graphic design RafamateoStudio
Translation and proofreading George Hutton
Cover photograph Maxime Delvaux
Lithography Rovira Digital, Barcelona
Print agpograf impressors, Barcelona

First published by
Verlag der Buchhandlung Walther und Franz König
Ehrenstrasse 4
D-50672 Köln
verlag@buchhandlung-walther-koenig.de

Printed in Spain
ISBN: 978-3-7533-0191-4

Distribution

Germany, Austria and Switzerland
Buchhandlung Walther König, Cologne
Tel. +49 (0) 221 / 20 59 6-53
Fax +49 (0) 221 / 20 59 6-60
verlag@buchhandlung-walther-koenig.de

Distribution outside the United States and Canada, Germany, Austria and Switzerland
Thames & Hudson Ltd., London
www.thamesandhudson.com

United States and Canada
D.A.P. / Distributed Art Publishers, Inc., New York
www.artbook.com

Contents

4 **[Play]**
Moritz Küng

12 **A New Internationalism**
Sam Chermayeff

16 **Apartment for Nacho, Barcelona**

22 **Luz House, Cilleros**

32 **Luz House II, Madrid**

42 **Acne Studios, Nagoya**

50 **Acne Studios, Stockholm**

58 **Llacuna Residential Building, Barcelona**

68 **Acne Studios, New York**

76 **Acne Studios, Paris**

82 **Praga Residential Building, Barcelona**

92 **Verdi House, Barcelona**

106 **Costa House, Barcelona**

118 **Quinta da Ponte, Sintra**

Tenant House

Garage and Groundskeeper's House

136 **Patio House, Aiguablava**

140 **House in Collserola, Barcelona**

144 **Apartamento Headquarters, Barcelona**

149 **Nexus**

A Voice through Others' Voices
Arquitectura-G

Moritz Küng

Just as I was beginning to write this text about the Barcelona-based collective Arquitectura-G, founded in 2006 by Jonathan Arnabat, Jordi Ayala-Bril, Aitor Fuentes and Igor Urdampilleta, I found myself in the company of Aitor and Igor on a brief tour around three of their housing projects in Barcelona, all of which were completed in 2021. We went to the Praga Residential Building, in the Horta district; the Llacuna Residential Building in Poble Nou, a stone's throw from the shore; and the Costa House near the Putxet Park in the city's upper district. At one point, I was standing on the first floor of the Praga building (named after its street, like the other two), in the master bedroom of the vacant duplex apartment, and I looked out of the French window. What I saw surprised me, not so much because of the view and scenery, but because of the sight that

Moritz Küng is an independent exhibition curator, critic and editor based in Barcelona, working at the intersection of visual art, architecture and artist book publishing. He is currently working on the comprehensive exhibition and catalogue project *Blank. Raw. Illegible... Artists' Books as Statement (1960-2020)*, to be inaugurated in 2023 at the Leopold-Hoesch-Museum, Düren (Germany). Recent articles have been published in: Espejo, Bea (ed.), *Ignasi Aballí. Corrección* (Madrid: Turner, 2022); Bodman, Sarah (ed.), *The Artist's Book Yearbook 2022–2023* (Bristol: Impact Press, 2022); De Vylder, Jan and Prandi, Annamaria (eds.), *Seven Questions* (Zurich/Berlin: ETH/Ruby Press, 2022).

unfolded before me, in layers. My gaze wandered ahead, over the neat, narrow and recently planted greenery of the patio garden, and towards its outer end, straight back to the main entrance where we had accessed the complex (that is, through the rod lattice gates on the ground floor and the parapets of the short access-bridges above, that lead to the apartments on either side of the U-shaped plan). My eyes were drawn outwards, to the steep side street, before finally taking in the average-looking 1980s neighbouring building.

I am fully aware that my clumsy description of this particular moment is somewhat hazy and may indeed sound rather confusing, but my inside-out gaze was a multi-layered experience: the "looking out" turned into a "looking inside", and my "overlooking" eventually became "looking through" the architecture. Right there, I had an epiphany.

At that moment, when I suddenly understood this very feature of the building's design, I was convinced that Arquitectura-G must be outstanding architects. But I also wondered—given the little I knew about the collective's work—how a photographer could possibly capture and frame such an "expanded" yet ephemeral "act of seeing". Architecture is now disseminated faster and more intensely than ever, and today's architects are communicating (and vying for attention) more and more, via publications, monographs, catalogues, websites and social media platforms. Thus, the "image"—pragmatic, seductive, truthful, manipulative, euphemistic, etc.—has long ceased to be innocent, and has instead become increasingly decisive for the "business".

[Rewind]

I only recently learned about Arquitectura-G's work through their first monograph, *Nineteen Interventions*, published in 2019 by Apartamento. This publishing house is known for its everyday-life interior magazine of the same name—a kind of anti-gloss, but all the more glam-grunge—to which Arquitectura-G also regularly contribute, reviewing particular houses that appeal to them (e.g. by Ricardo Bofill, Fernando Higueras, César Manrique, Anne Holtrop, Office Kersten Geers David Van Severen, Smiljan Radić, Kazuo Shinohara). *Nineteen Interventions* brings together the most telling projects of the collective's first decade, encompassing their furniture, refurbishments, apartment renovations and the extensions that rest upon the framework of existing buildings.

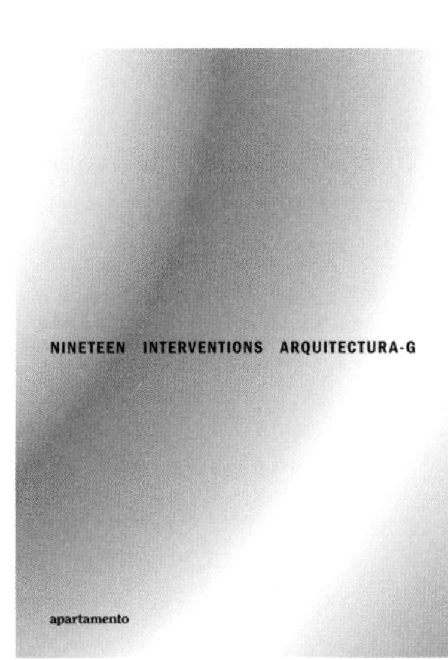

The book made a mark on me in various ways, and not only because of its oversized format (36.3 × 25.8 cm) or the thought-provoking reference to "interventions" in its title (a term primarily used in the art context, emphasising a more fleeting state of being), but also because it is pretty difficult to classify. I'm kind of hooked on artists'

books—that is, books made (and often published) by artists as a work of *art* in their own right—so, some time ago, I started to look out for a similar typology or phenomenon among architecture books. The architectural equivalent of an artist's book, i.e. an "architect's book", would be about a singular architectural practice; it would not only document the work, but also emphasise or embody the book itself as a *piece of architecture* in its own right.[1] That said, and bearing in mind my own limited knowledge of the field, I have come across many potential candidates, but only a handful of publications that really could be categorised as such.[2]

Unlike most architecture monographs, *Nineteen Interventions* strictly separates pictures and drawings into two self-contained sections. First, there is an uninterrupted sequence of more than 100 full-bleed colour images by photographer José Hevia, and this is then followed by nineteen sets of floor plans, masterfully juxtaposed with a section or an elevation. Although the abundant chronology of images unfortunately lacks descriptive captions, the plans are individually reproduced on double spreads (obstructed, however, by the book's gutter) and complemented with corresponding key data about the project in question. This main bulk is then "framed" by two shorter texts at the beginning and end of the book, as conceptual brackets: firstly, architect Oscar Tusquets ponders his earliest encounter with the collective when they celebrated their Mies van der Rohe Award for Emerging Architects in 2015; then, critic Moisés Puente compares their monograph concept with Raymond Queneau's *Exercises in Style* (1947), in which the same trivial and everyday story is written ninety-nine times, each in a different style. As an epilogue, architect and designer Sam Chermayeff emphasises the collective's profound sensibility for materials and the spirit of the site as a "playboy modernism without the hubris". The shiny silver Chromolux cover, with black titles printed in matt (on the front and, tellingly, mirrored on the back), strongly hints at the alleged hedonistic nature of Arquitectura-G's projects. All in all, *Nineteen Interventions* was a hybrid between a design magazine, photo-book and architect monograph, in which Hevia's signature photography took centre-stage.

A continuous stream of impressions, spaces, views, textures and surfaces merge and intersect side-by-side, creating a visual amalgam. Hevia's architectural framing is largely determined by central perspectives with a focus on surfaces and lighting, and he creates visual overlaps with adjacent spaces. He successfully captures and implements the architects' supposed vocabulary, which is equally rooted in and based upon plain stylistic principles such as simple geometric shapes and volumes, material-inherent surfaces and a mildly contrasting colour palette. However, I couldn't help but get the impression that the photographer created "architecture" anew, so to speak, by himself, and according to his own vision.[3] Although Hevia's approach, in the way it highlights the diversity of surfaces, seems to be completely in sync with the nature of Arquitectura-G's projects, it was only later that I discovered that it's not all about superficiality.

1 — Küng, Moritz, "The Architecture of Books on Architecture", in Puente, Moisés (ed.), *Quaderns d'Arquitectura i Urbanisme*, no. 270 (*Europa Europa*), Barcelona, 2018, pp. 123-132.

2 — b&k+ [Arno Brandlhuber and Bernd Kniess], *Tiere + Deine Freunde*, Cologne: self-published, 2001 (10 × 10 cm, 16 pp., ills. colour, staple-bound, edition of ca. 50 copies); and De Vylder, Jan and Vinck, Inge, *Verveling/Gallery Magazine*, no. 1, Ghent: APE–Art Paper Editions, 2020 (curated by Jonathan Robert Maj and Johannes Ströhmenger, 23 × 29.7 cm, 160 pp., ills. colour, paperback + poster, edition of 1,000 copies).

3 — Many photographers implement their own artistic views in the recording or documentation of architects' buildings. Think, for example, about the more outspoken positions of Thomas Ruff and his art photography for the Swiss Herzog & de Meuron, in which he digitally enhanced, manipulated or even "white-washed" the original material to achieve a conceptually more coherent result (*Haus Nr. 4 II* [Ricola Laufen], 1991); the many diptychs by Walter Nierdermayr for SANAA that are part of his long-standing and ongoing series *Bildraum* and which are as rigorously composed as Hevia's pictures, but capturing above all the key ephemeral quality of their novel buildings; the imminent cinematographic staging in Hans Werlemann's images for some of OMA's projects (e.g. the giraffe appearing at Villa dall'Ava, Paris, 1991); or the infamous interior views by Philippe Ruault of Lacaton & Vassal's House at Coutras (2000) in which the disorderly everyday life of the residents is captured in a most unorthodox, scrupulous way (underwear included). Interestingly, and regarding the latter, José Hevia re-photographed the Apartment for Nacho in 2016, i.e. an early project of Arquitectura-G that he had first documented in 2012. While the first series just shows the completed but uninhabited apartment, the second series revealed how rigorously the client had appropriated the space with his own belongings.

[Fast-forward]

So, standing there in the bedroom with Aitor and Igor on that rather hot and muggy afternoon, and looking out of the window, my early scepticism was soon blown away. The Praga Residential Building's entrance hall emphasises, with its "single-column-portico", a traditional yet highly sculptural typology. The monumental-looking, centred volume conceals the stairway to the upper-level apartments on the 2nd and 3rd floor. Narrow rod lattice gates, on either side, mark the boundary between the street's public space and the semi-public access to all the apartments. In turn, two additional gates allow exclusive access to the patio/terraces of the two duplex units on the ground floor. The interplay between the public and the private, or the extrovert and the intimate, is consequently imposed in the subdivision of each of the units; within its very centre (along the patio) is the open kitchen, and at the outer ends are the more private rooms on the upper levels, such as the double-height living room of the duplex with its narrow and high windows, two metres above the ground. Although the architects reflected the densely built neighbourhood in their approach, they also created an extraordinarily liveable quality, by means of a grand gesture (i.e. the inwardly folded façade) and a highly compact zoning (portico-access-courtyard). The only thing missing is a swimming pool on the spacious roof; unfortunately, it was abandoned for cost reasons, as Aitor and Igor remarked.

While the façades of the Praga project are immaculately rendered in white lime, those of the Llacuna Residential Building are kept in light earthy tones, also in lime render. This five-story building, with two shops, six apartments and a penthouse, is located on a "clipped" corner, a characteristic typology of Barcelona's urban blocks. Its irregular pentagonal plot, with a small interior garden attached on the rear, has been radically split into two halves. The very centre of the plan is occupied by a grand spiral staircase that functions as a "hinge". Gently set back from the street, the cylindrical space is flooded by natural light from the top and the side. The access area—as an adjoining space that often gets neglected by many architects—is once again dealt with as a key concern in this project. The communal entrance is marked by a narrow, slim slit in the façade, and it extends over two and a half floors. If you go up the stairs (instead of taking the lift), you pass two split levels with loggia-like "outposts". They don't necessarily have a purpose, apart from letting in daylight and improving ventilation. However, as rather diffuse but protective spaces, they add a sublime quality and invite you to pause as you go up, probably to ponder urban life. The generously dimensioned spiral staircase determines many small details (such as the custom-made concave letterboxes in the entrance hall), especially the *Raumplan* itself of the penthouse. It is twice as big as the apartments underneath, and all the rooms here are grouped around the central cylinder which results in a continuum of spaces. When entering via the staircase (or from the lift), you can get straight to the kitchen, living room, bathroom or rear bedroom(s). A mezzanine on either half of the staircase nestles up against its unique round wall.

The idea of contiguous, continual spaces (Adolf Loos)—rooms, anterooms, terraces, patio, garden—reaches its conceptual peak in the Costa House, a townhouse for a single family. An average rectangular plot has been occupied with an L-shaped, two-story volume that leaves ample space for a garden at the rear. The two façades (at the front and back) could not be more different. Seen from the street, the house appears to be hermetically sealed. Besides the blind front door—with two covers of technical cabinets next to it, and the two slim windows of the first floor with plain steel shutters—only the indentations of the joints are really apparent, in such a way that the façade is reduced to a smooth, plain white surface. Just three elements give the façade a certain plasticity: there is a small-but-distinctive canopy above the front door, which not only offers protection from the weather but also provides daylight for the narrow hallway behind it; on the right, there is the intercom, along with the house number custom-made of white-painted bent tubular steel, protruding from the wall; and finally, on the top of the building, a thin white marble slab protrudes discreetly, covering the technical units of the roof terrace behind. In contrast to the "non-façade" at the front, the rear is "non-existing", as it were. Coming from the hallway, the space literally opens up. The generous living room (which corresponds to the master bedroom on the first floor) is directly connected to the garden and the adjacent, slightly elevated floor of the kitchen area (which in turn corresponds to a bathroom and a study upstairs). On the façade, the rooms' large sliding doors—finished off with white curtains and net railings—can be fully opened. As a result, the boundaries between inside and outside, the atrium and interiors, all dissolve, and the house thus turns into a breezy, light-filled porch.

[Pause]

These recent projects reveal concerns that seem to have been at the heart of Arquitectura-G's work from the outset, such as "how to divide a space without making divisions", as they themselves ponder. One of the collective's early works was the Apartment for Nacho (2012), just 150 square metres in size. It no longer exists in its original form, but, in retrospect, it seems to encompass the key elements that the architects would later develop on larger scales. In this "blueprint", the term used in their monograph, "intervention" comes into play most appropriately. The architects converted a semi-basement (with two central columns and an adjoining smaller room) into a habitable flat, with only a few (but significant) separations and adjustments. As well as stripping the flat down, and installing a new terracotta floor, two large windows with sliding doors at the rear, a kitchen, and a shower with a toilet, the architects proposed just two elements in order to strategically structure and subdivide the given space. First of all, on the opposite side to the entrance door and along the wall orthogonal to the façade, they placed an elongated, almost room-high volume to serve as a dressing room/storage space (which

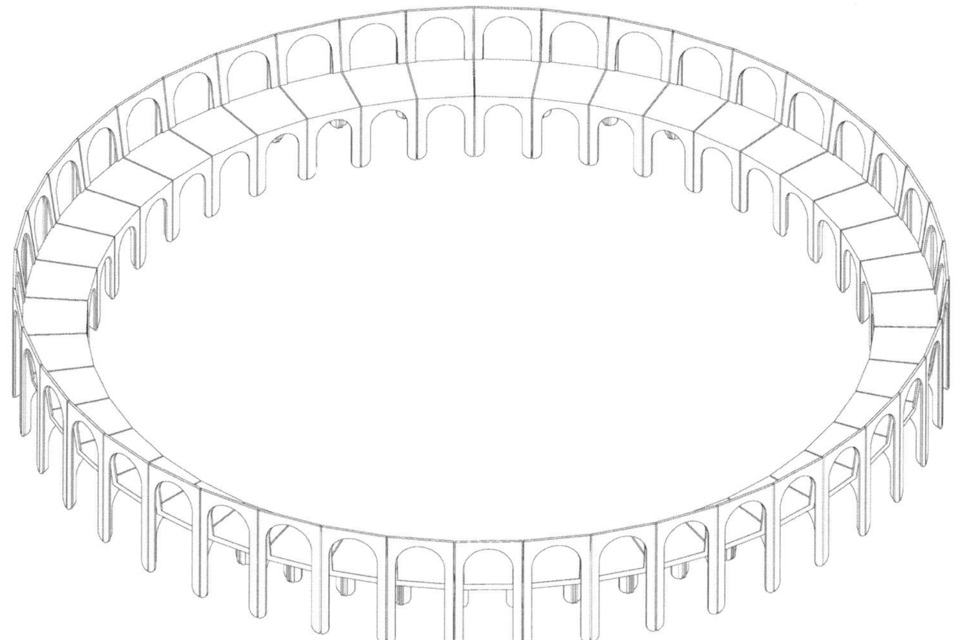

Claudio chair arrangement as the Coloseum.

Claudio and Claudia chairs, 2012.
Photograph: © José Hevia

also accentuated the location of the small bathroom). Secondly, they positioned a free-standing, right-angled wall element between the two columns, creating a more private area with a bed. Both elements were panelled with pristine white glossy tiles, the bedroom with a mirror. In fact, they structure the space gently, without strict divisions, ultimately resulting in a fluid spatial continuum.

Around the same time, Arquitectura-G also launched, through their own brand Indoors, their first furniture designs: the black or white powder-coated steel chair, Claudio (2012)—also available in stainless steel—as well as two derivatives as a children's chair, i.e. Claudia (2012), and the Claudio Side Table (2016). With arches cut out on each side, this architectural miniature is somehow reminiscent of the iconic Palazzo della Civiltà Italiana in Rome (also known as the "Square Colosseum", a rationalist building erected under Mussolini which today houses the headquarters of Fendi). In these designs, that monumental cubic block seems to be reinterpreted on a domestic scale, with subtle details. While the lower part of each leg is rounded to rests on a single point, the back has a double arch (a small one for the inclined backrest, and an elongated one for the upright rear end). If 43 of these chairs were lined up, they would form a perfect circle due to the seat's trapezoidal shape. The "categorically geometrical character of the piece," as the architects note on their website, "breaks the formal purity of the whole, giving in exchange a feigned illusion of a vanishing point, in the way of forced perspectives as in the Renaissance, or the [*Pittura metafisica*] paintings of Giorgio de Chirico."

[Play]

After the site visits, we went back to Arquitectura-G's studio, near the Llacuna project. Aitor and Igor further discussed and commented on a recent collaboration with the Swedish fashion house Acne Studio, which has a presence on four continents, in a total of 64 brand stores. Many of them were realised by Acne's in-house design team, but Arquitectura-G has also been involved, remodelling —in collaboration with British furniture designer Max Lamb and French lightning engineer Benoit Lalloz—four shops (thus far) in Nagoya (2019), Stockholm (2020), New York (2021) and Paris (2022). Rumour has it that Acne's acronym once stood for "Associated Computer Nerd Enterprises" but that it later changed to "Ambition to Create Novel Expressions" —the latter iteration could also apply to Arquitectura-G's own ambitions. As it turns out, many of the collective's earlier concepts for the shops resonate or have indeed been further developed. They simultaneously combine roughness with delicacy, high-tech with low-tech, chaos with order, playfulness with rigour, hard materials with smooth ones, precision-cut with handcrafted elements, imitations with vintage, inspirations found on site with ideas suggested by their client (Jonny Johansson, co-founder and creative director of Acne Studio).

A crucial factor is that the architects' design solutions primarily evolve from model-making, often on the rather unusually large scale of 1:20. The role of coincidences, mistakes or even accidents during their work process should not be played down: "We don't imagine that the model represents what the store will become, but the store will become what there is in the model. It is a process of representation opposite to the usual."[4] Such a slip-up occurred, for example, in the simulation of the wire-bent metal clothes-rails in the model for the Nagoya store: their wavy imperfections were directly transferred into reality. Later, they were even reused for the shop in Paris, where the bespoke hand-made hangers became a self-referential "conversation piece".

For outsiders, though, Arquitectura-G's store designs are difficult to distinguish from those made by Acne's team. However, all four shops consist of compellingly authentic solutions and unique spheres. They are cool and sophisticated: the Nagoya branch has thin, curved, precision-cut partition walls made of brushed stainless steel, combined with greyish plush carpeting and a contrasting shotcrete technical ceiling. In the New York store, there are pale water-green painted walls that take up the hue of the translucent, sandblasted glass panels of the nine triangular fitting rooms (which strategically subdivide the surface of the two merged store-units and visually hide a structural wall breach). They are elegant and sober too: in Stockholm, there are three interconnected halls (those of the former Credit Bank branch, infamous for the robbery and resulting "Stockholm Syndrome") that combine original Ekeberg and faux marble (on the floor, and respectively painted on the columns) with new marble stones (for superimposed floor tiles, low display

4 — www.youtube.com/watch?v=7N-MFvsV0F60&ab_channel=AcneStudios.

podia-slabs, and an added false colonnade). In Paris, the 19th-century façade's Saint-Maximin limestone was used for the entire interior as well (i.e. the two floors and cladded walls), in an attempt to dissolve the boundary between the outside and the inside.

[Pause]

All of Arquitectura-G's recent works, as discussed here, reveal a quality that should not be underestimated: that of concealing things. Their effortless, thorough and sober executions seem to successfully absorb local building regulations, given the visual environmental noise or other such obstacles. Now in the midst of their second decade, Arquitectura-G repeatedly try out new, fresh ideas that keep us guessing about what's coming next.

A New Internationalism

Sam Chermayeff

As a discipline, architecture is referential when it would often prefer not to be. At this moment, we are beholden to the past and we avoid nostalgia. We are not, as yet, in a new internationalism. Dominant culture is still just that. And we are not experiencing a rebirth. We are, quite understandably, clinging onto various principles —not least Modernism, which is now into its second century. In other words, a dominant canon has been well defined, and architecture is playing around with it.

Arquitectura-G understands these implied definitions without worship. They understand Modernism in so many of its iterations. At first, their practice was concerned with how the universal would fit into the specific contexts of their projects, so their commissions and resulting buildings addressed the surroundings and existing tectonics. Their walls were invariably massive. People lived within structure, both constructively and programmatically.

Sam Chermayeff is an architect, designer and teacher. Sam trained in architecture at the University of Texas at Austin and the Architectural Association, London. He is a founding partner and director in the architecture firm June 14 Meyer-Grohbrügge & Chermayeff and Sam Chermayeff Office. The studios have offices in New York and Berlin, and they work on a wide range of design-driven projects, including large multiunit residential buildings in Berlin, several small houses in New York, and furniture all over. Sam began his architectural career at SANAA / Kazuyo Sejima + Ryue Nishizawa, where, for over five years, he worked on an array of projects across built and curatorial work, including the 2009 Serpentine Pavilion and the 2010 Venice Architecture Biennale.

Arquitectura-G has created a body of work that, despite being inherently and intentionally local, appeals beyond its context. On these pages, they chart their trajectory to date: we see how, ever since their beginnings, they have sought to tell new truths and stories in such a way that even the specifics of their work can feel universal. Here, we find projects built across Europe, the US and Japan, all of which are a conscious expansion of their practice and thinking. The Acne store in Japan, for example, is decidedly Japanese. It overtly deals with, uses and addresses Japanese construction and, by extension, Japanese culture. And yet, it is not a reference, per se, to something we know. It is a small, precise contribution to an increasingly globalised canon. That is, the office and their work here represent at least two truths, as well as any possible connections that might arise between them.

The notion of bringing together disparate design ideas is a core aspect of Arquitectura-G's work, including concepts not necessarily of their own invention: they are tacitly interested in foreign ideas of universality, combined with (or imported into) the Spanish context. The very best of Modernism and Arquitectura-G's work do this intentionally. By way of example, Arquitectura-G designs buildings with details wherein we can read gravity in relation to materiality. This creates atmospheres that are both heavy and light at the same time.

Arquitectura-G is pushing the fundamentals of materiality perhaps because architecture, as a discipline, is somewhat disoriented at the moment. Theirs is a methodology on material, rather than a celebration. Our teachers were modernists, and our idols are stars. There are no universally accepted answers: we can no longer apply a set language to any situation. In this way, Arquitectura-G discovered that something cannot be lost when it is taken out of context. Take the Japanese studio SANAA as an example: their work is clearly beloved by Arquitectura-G, as can be seen in these pages. They built the New Museum in New York and the Rolex Learning Center at the EPFL in Lausanne, two buildings that take their programmatic design from their briefs and context, but are still distinctly foreign objects in their surroundings. Both of these projects are wonderful, specifically because they stand aside quite so elegantly. They are very much about their purposes: the Rolex Learning Center, to use Sejima's words, is a "softly divided" public space that allows a vast community to come together in different ways. As a parti and model it is a careful observation of Lausanne and the EPFL; meanwhile, as a language, with its thin columns, white industrial surfaces and delicate mullions (and so on), it is the sheer embodiment of SANAA. By contrast, Arquitectura-G have understood in their own work (and perhaps, by extension, in all the work that they are drawn to) that their language can be more flexible, yet still very much theirs, while also retaining its signature truth.

At the time of writing, Arquitectura-G and Sam Chermayeff Office happen to be working together on a project, namely a showroom for the Italian company Flos. It is a remarkably easy collaboration insomuch that we understand each other. This is not to say that we always agree: we vigorously debate many things, often the unseen. Even though this is a joint project, it fully embraces Arquitectura-G's notion of unpretentious material honesty. It is steel, and comes at a price, but it is also casual and quite fun. It is a paper model (and its failings) scaled up. Steel plate is doing what the paper was doing at 1 to 20, bending a bit. The project's Dutch context remains unclear at present, but its own materiality is pushed to its natural limit. Despite its small size, it is a globalised project: it merges at least four cultures.

In thinking about Arquitectura-G's oeuvre, we see the intellectual profits of Cadaqués, a coastal village in Catalonia. Here, Modernism met vernacular in unexpected ways: it is 20th-century architecture manifested as an exchange, one that is newly relevant in the 21st century. There is a subtle but radical difference from the contemporaneous Bauhaus in America, which burst onto the scene in the form of proposals for a brand-new future. In Cadaqués (inspired in part by Josep Lluís Sert), José Antonio Coderch, Harnden & Bombelli, Correa Milá, Ivan Chermayeff, Oscar Tusquets, Lluís Clotet and others repurposed existing house typologies into buildings that connect their history with exuberant post-war living. These architects changed the existing buildings dramatically. For a start, they put bedrooms downstairs and living spaces upstairs, where the views are. Somewhere along the way they borrowed a vernacular idea from the island of Ibiza, where wood was pricier than masonry: by extension, it was easier to build sofas, desks, counters (and so on) into/with the stone structure. This nearly ancient structural-cum-spatial idea became the foundation for a particular strain of modern design, and much later it would form the basis for Arquitectura-G's earliest projects. This merging of programme (a bench/handrail, for example) and structure is the foundation of their way of thinking, and has since been greatly expanded. In Cadaqués and Arquitectura-G's work alike, we find a kind of universalism that stems from the specific: in the studio's most recent work, a series of external inputs are applied to a very small place, as a reimagining of the original amalgamation. The result is something clear and solid, unlike the open mess of 21st-century globalisation.

As with all great architecture, the work here looks easy to conceive because it is "natural", in the way that Germans say "*natürlich*" to mean "of course", such as when a wall becomes a handrail that carries a bench. In Paris, for example, Arquitectura-G worked with one particular kind of local stone. This is not interesting in and of itself (it is quite a common approach), but in this case it implies that the Paris context is in fact international, i.e. not an exclusively French commodity. That is, they suggest that both the stone and the project belong to the larger Western culture. Arquitectura-G applies the unmistakeably Parisian stone to the walls, shelves and doors in such a way that we, almost without noticing, think of these elements typologically and not contextually. They do this while also ensuring that the stone remains true to itself. We understand, without fetishisation, that there are not many pieces of metal hiding behind it to make it work. Stone, which is good in compression and makes excellent surfaces, is doing what we technically and intuitively understand it to be doing, as it once did in Ibiza and many other places.

Arquitectura-G set out, I believe consciously, to find a way of building and detailing that is universal and yet specific on several levels. This is perhaps not a new observation; their earliest work hints at this possibility, in that we see vernacular made modern, with no contradiction, when contradiction is so often seen as a virtue within architecture. In other words, their work artfully holds onto everything, while still making sense as a coherent whole. "Everything", in this case, refers to the context of their projects, such as the materiality and weight of a Swedish bank; it means the notion of Modernism, and that we are roughly all the same, and it also encompasses the Spanish-ness of a practice. Their newer projects, the proof of these multiple truths, promise architecture that complements rather than compromises.

Arquitectura-G's way of working is relevant to an open question facing the discipline at present, i.e. the assertion that architecture, in the European context, is based on a very long history of wealth and extraction. This is not news to much of the world, but privileged contexts (Europe, America and Japan, among others) and the profession of architecture are both famously slow to adapt.

The methodology evident in these pages is part of a fresh awakening to the fact that the dominant cultural canon can be exclusionary, at the expense of the different. It is unclear how to change this situation. Arquitectura-G, perhaps even to its surprise, offer a way forward: their work, on its current trajectory and due to the collective's methodology, is able to hear voices that often get ignored. They can take loud voices and calmly quiet them down, while amplifying others. This means that they can be sustainable with a sense of humility, or build in contexts far (literally or metaphorically) from their own, with respect rather than homage. They elucidate the potential in diversity and inclusivity as an asset, when the prevailing dogma might consider different perspectives as confusing or destabilising. Their approach is to make sense of difference, and expand possibilities.

Arquitectura-G have shifted their practice: now, there is always substantial crossover between their thinking, the project's context, the wider cultural context and issues of materiality. This melding of inputs might naturally cause the voice of the practice itself to recede. However, this is not the case. The realisation that their own voice and consistency can remain not just present but integral is a bold response to the predicament facing our entire profession.

Expanding possibilities from the perspective of wealth means employing humility as a tool. Their recent buildings in Barcelona—the Costa and Verdi houses, for example—are both closed and open. They are a combination of punched windows and retractable walls, with the qualities of both a fortress and public square. These contrasting conditions work together from an urban perspective and for the inhabitants. They draw on typology, how we understand houses in Barcelona, and how life can be reimagined. They are not funny or cute. They are, once again, multiple truths.

Apartment for Nacho, Barcelona

2011-2012

This is one of our first projects. Our friend Nacho had a photography studio with a back garden, and he wanted to convert it into a flat. The brief was pretty straightforward: he needed a space for sleeping, a space for cooking, and a bathroom. Money was tight, so the project came down to just a few strategic decisions; in the end, we created an L-shaped partition wall and a wardrobe, both covered in bright white tiles —these new elements redefined the whole space, creating distinct areas in order to meet the brief. Also, a new window onto the garden was installed, symmetrical to the existing one, and the floor was finished in red clay tiles. This layout, which divides the space without really dividing it, by simply generating little nooks as well as open areas, turned out to be perfect for Nacho's many house parties while he lived there —his apartment became a great place for bringing friends together.

Makeshift bar at one of Nacho's parties.
© Nacho Alegre

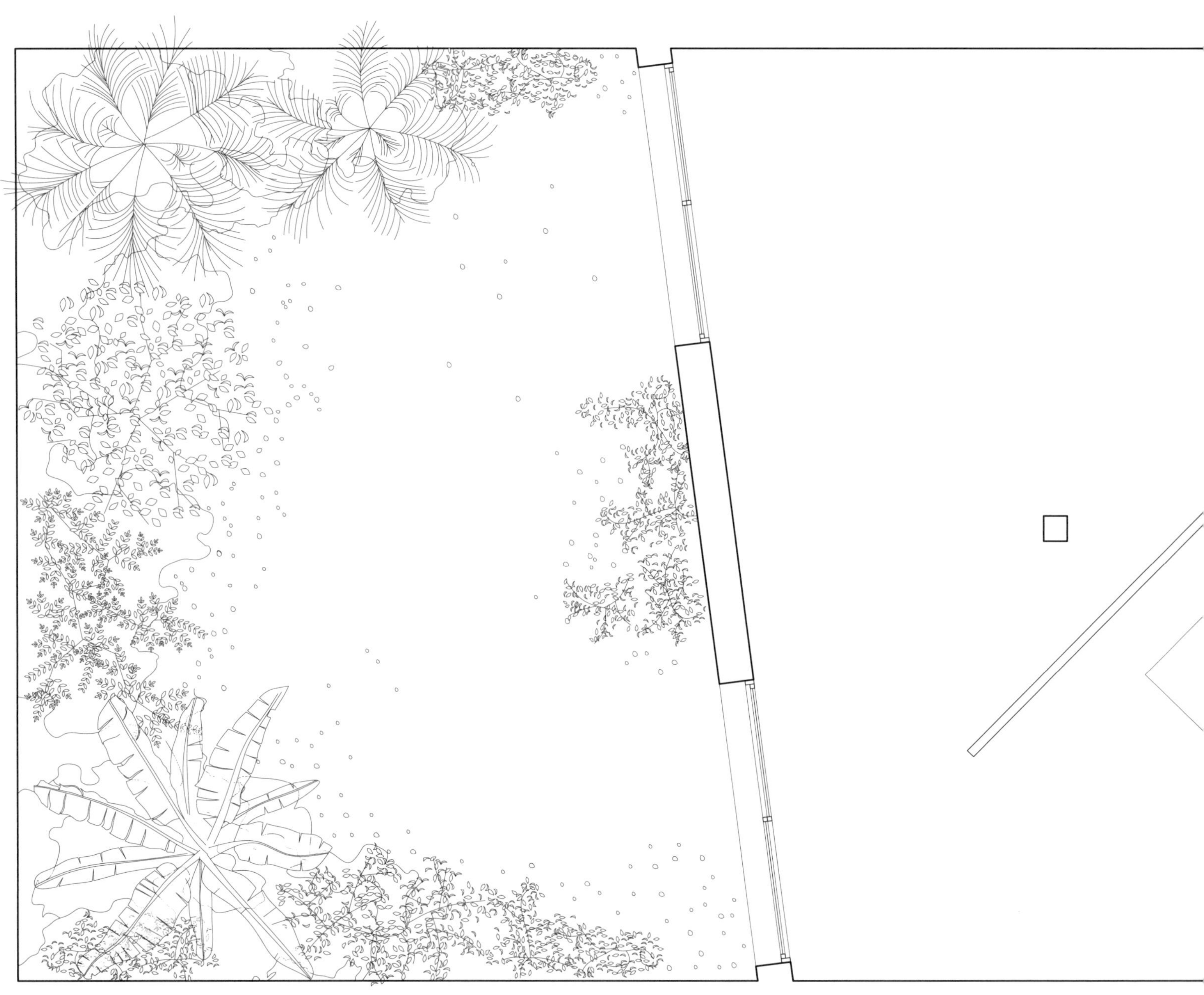

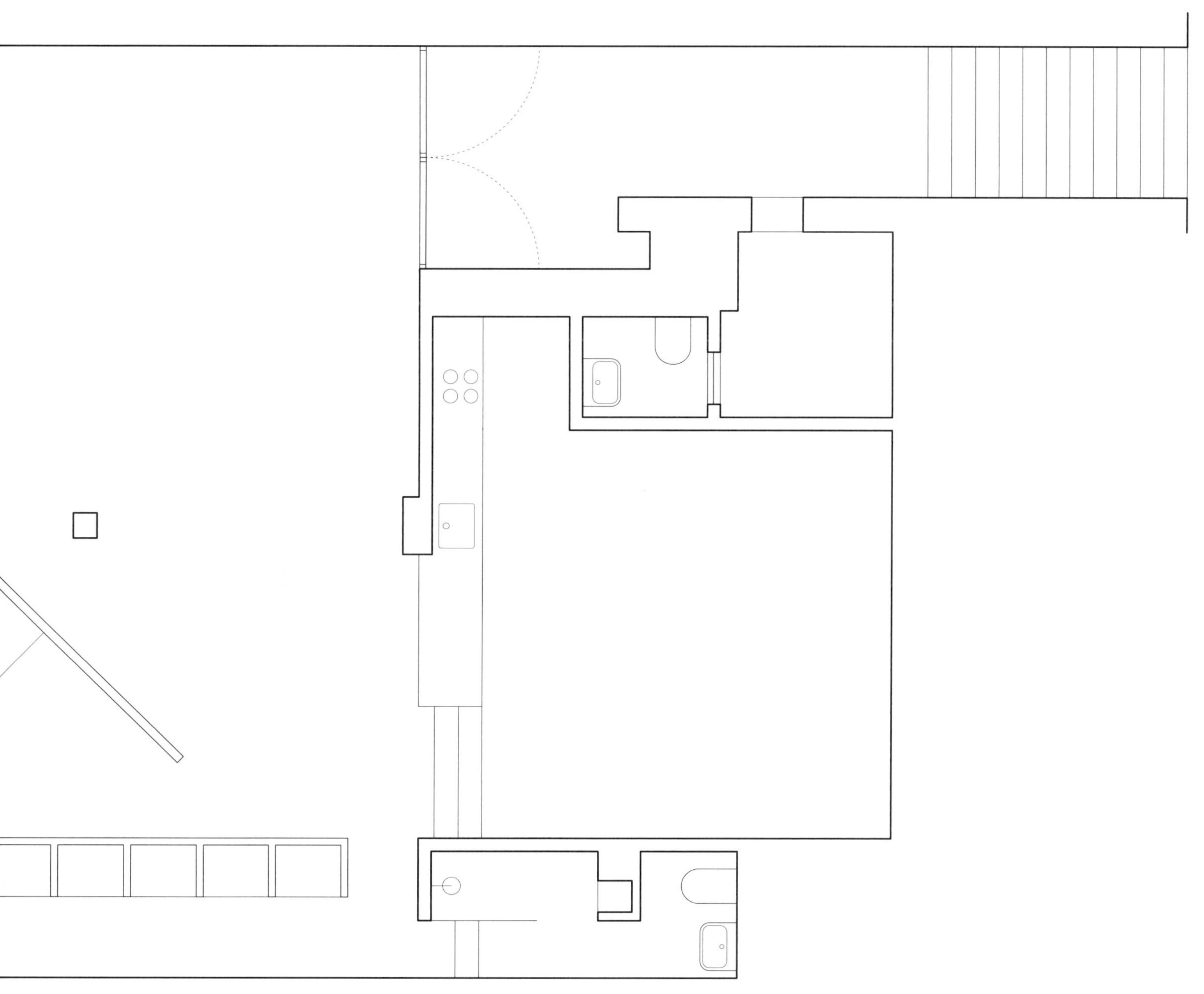

Luz House, Cilleros

2011-2013

Our client, Luz, wanted a restful place with a garden, somewhere not too far from Madrid. She found a house, nestled between party walls, and largely derelict—apart from the façades, which were in good condition—in Cilleros, a small village in Extremadura near the Portuguese border.

The interior of the house was completely stripped out, so we could then build two platforms around a central patio with a birch tree as its main feature. The openings in the two façades were uneven, so the floor structures had to be adjusted to fit, while the patio absorbed the remaining difference in levels.
The back half of the house offers views, and contains the kitchen and living room, which are crossed by the staircase. Meanwhile, the bedrooms open onto the main façade, and the ground floor is understood as a large shaded area, connecting the street with the garden.

In a house built on a low budget, the tree takes on the role of mediating between the different areas, as well as between the house and the sun. It acts as a screen between the common spaces and the bedrooms, and its foliage also protects the house from the sun in the summer, while letting in light during the winter. Furthermore, it gives the house an ever-changing ambience, with the passing of the seasons and the gentle ripple of its silvery leaves.

Garden at Luz House, 2015
© Adrià Cañameras

Luz House, Cilleros

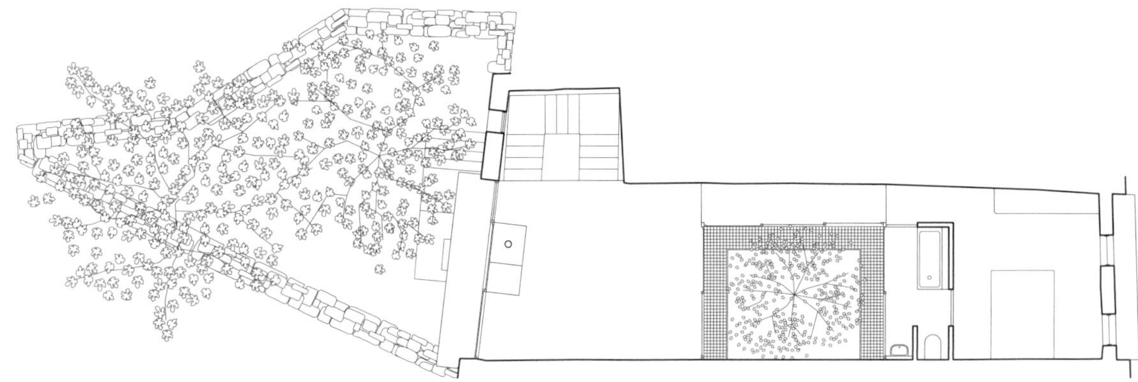
Second floor

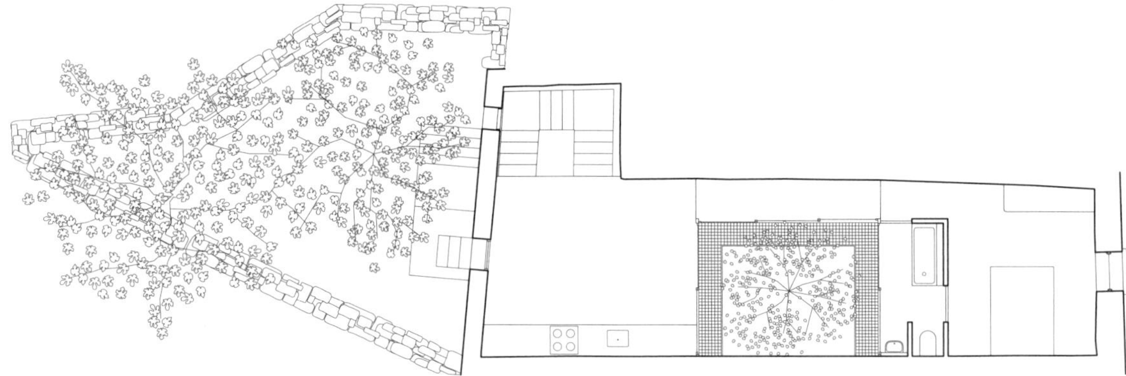
First floor

Ground floor

Luz House II, Madrid

2017-2018

In the film *The Swimmer* (1968), Ned Merrill (played by Burt Lancaster) is drinking a cocktail by the poolside, in the company of friends. He soon realises that there is a whole series of swimming pools, stretching all the way back to his own house. So, he decides to go home, but, instead of walking, he swims back from pool to pool.

Luz—the same client from Luz House—was still obsessed with the idea of inhabiting a garden. She kept looking for the right one, this time in Madrid itself, so she could set up her main residence there. She eventually found a ground-floor property within a residential building; it was connected to a garden containing the building's old laundry room, which was in a state of ruin. The ground floor space was not big enough to meet all the requirements of Luz's brief, so the laundry room would have to be taken over as well. As a result, the house was split in two, whereby you have to cross the garden to get from one part to the other. A swimming pool runs down the length of the garden, so the two sections of the house are connected by water.

During the construction phase, one of Luz's friends said to her: "A house split in two —that's mad! How are you going to get from one side to the other when it's raining?", to which she responded: "I'll swim!".

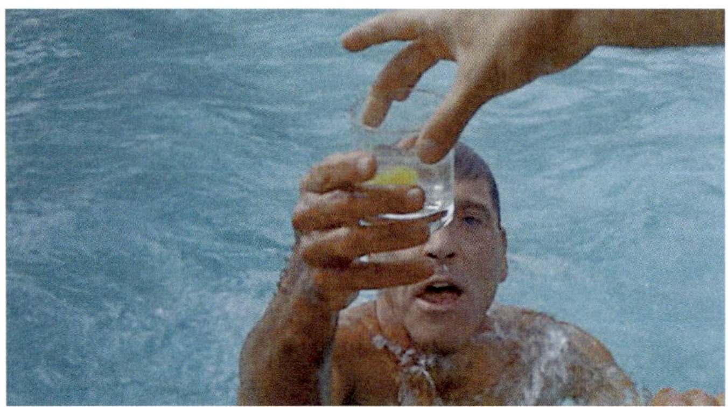

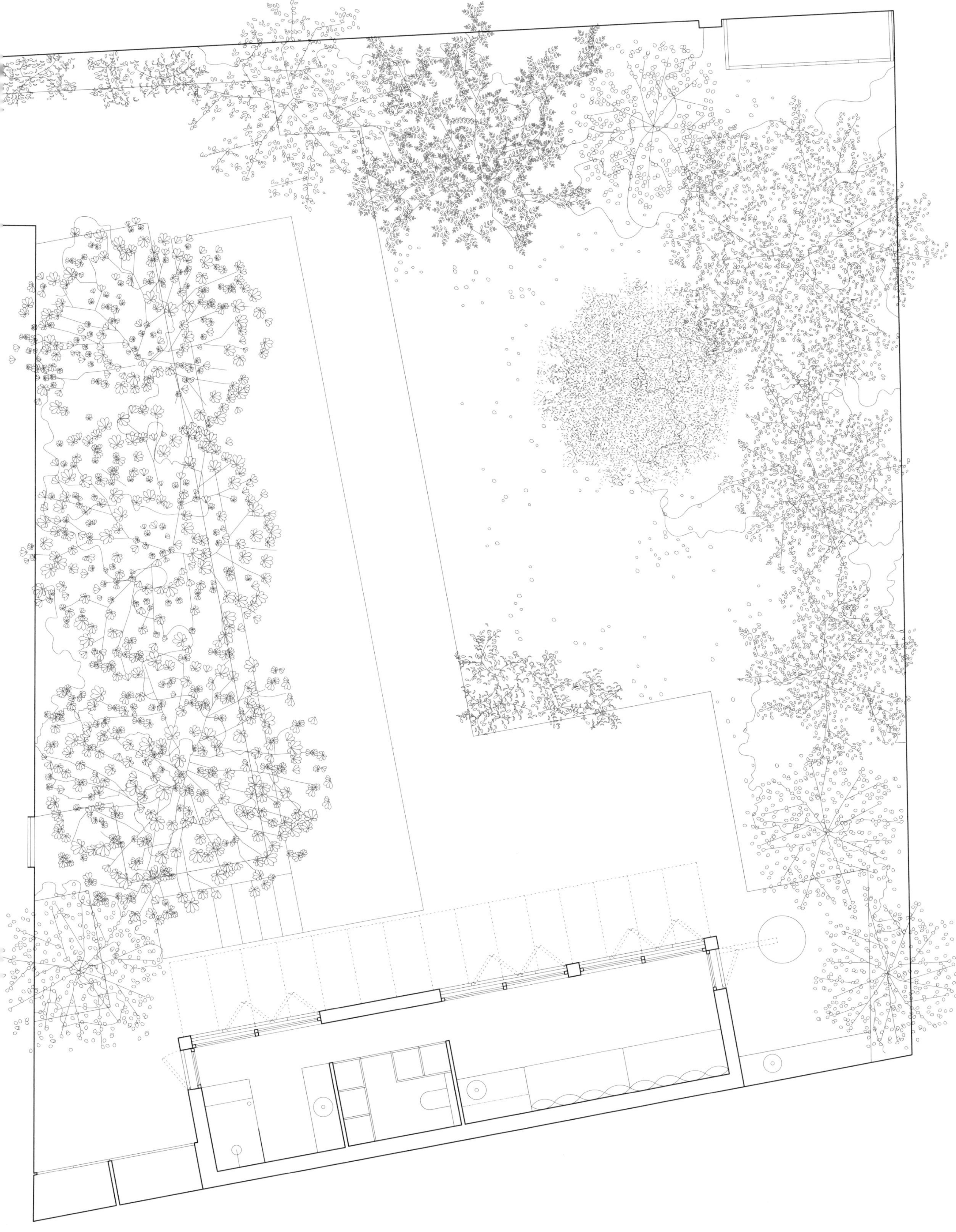

Luz House II, Madrid

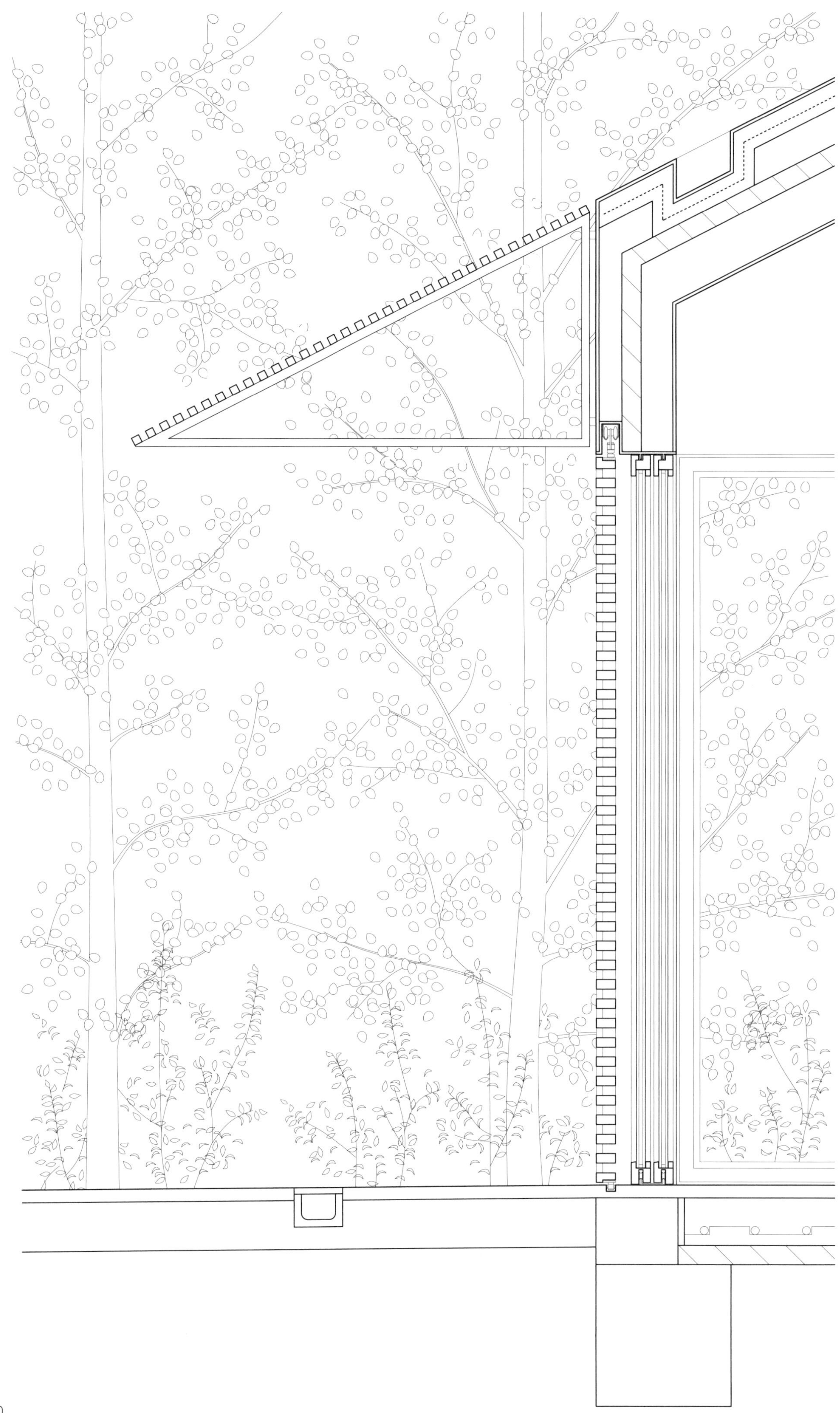

Acne Studios, Nagoya

2019

This project takes up the first floor of a glass-fronted building, on a main street in the city of Nagoya, Japan. It was our first project for Acne Studios, and the brief from Jonny Johansson (the brand's creative director) was to combine the DNA of Acne Studios with the strong local identity, while also bringing together high-tech and low-tech, an idea so prevalent in Japanese culture.

Three curved, 8-millimeter stainless-steel panels cut through the store, and mark out its various different uses: the commercial space, the fitting rooms and the back of house. Due to their geometry, these panels stand up without any supports, despite their near wafer-thinness. They rest upon a carpet of variable density, along with several podium-like seats emerging from it. The fireproofed pillars are left intact, as are the pre-existing cables and ceiling fittings. New hanging lights are installed, seeking a bold contrast between the raw and the delicate, between the rough and the sharp.

Villa Katsura, Kyoto, Japan. Lightweight panels divide the space.

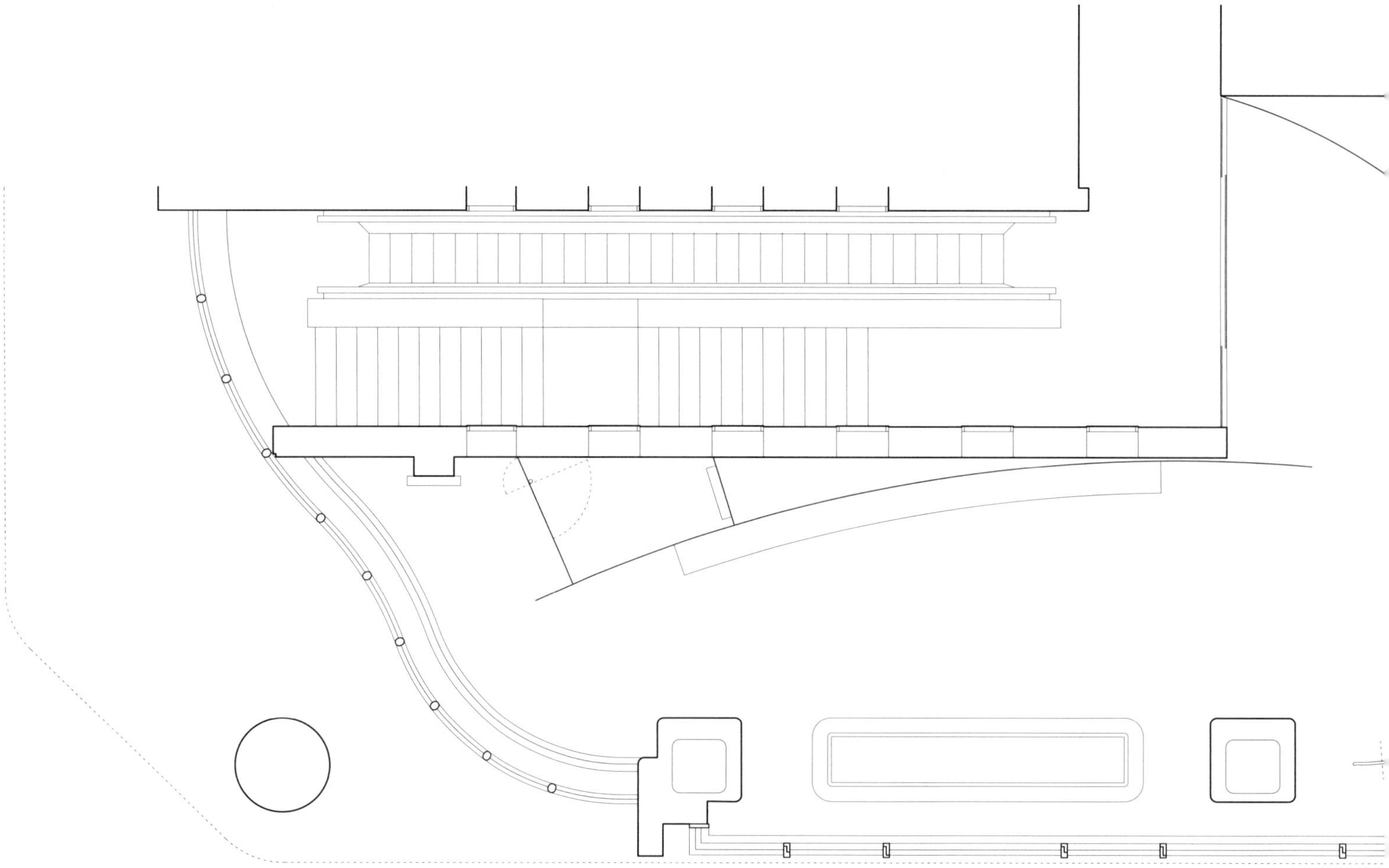

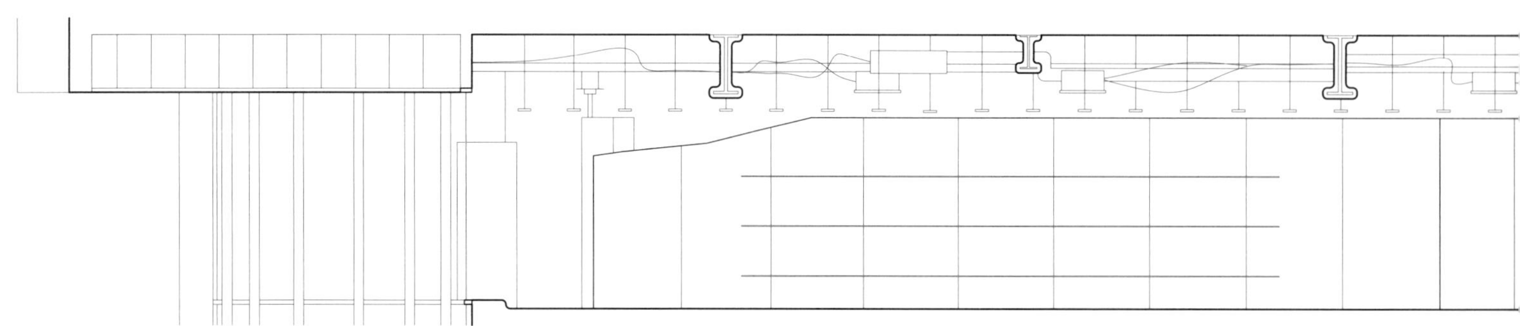

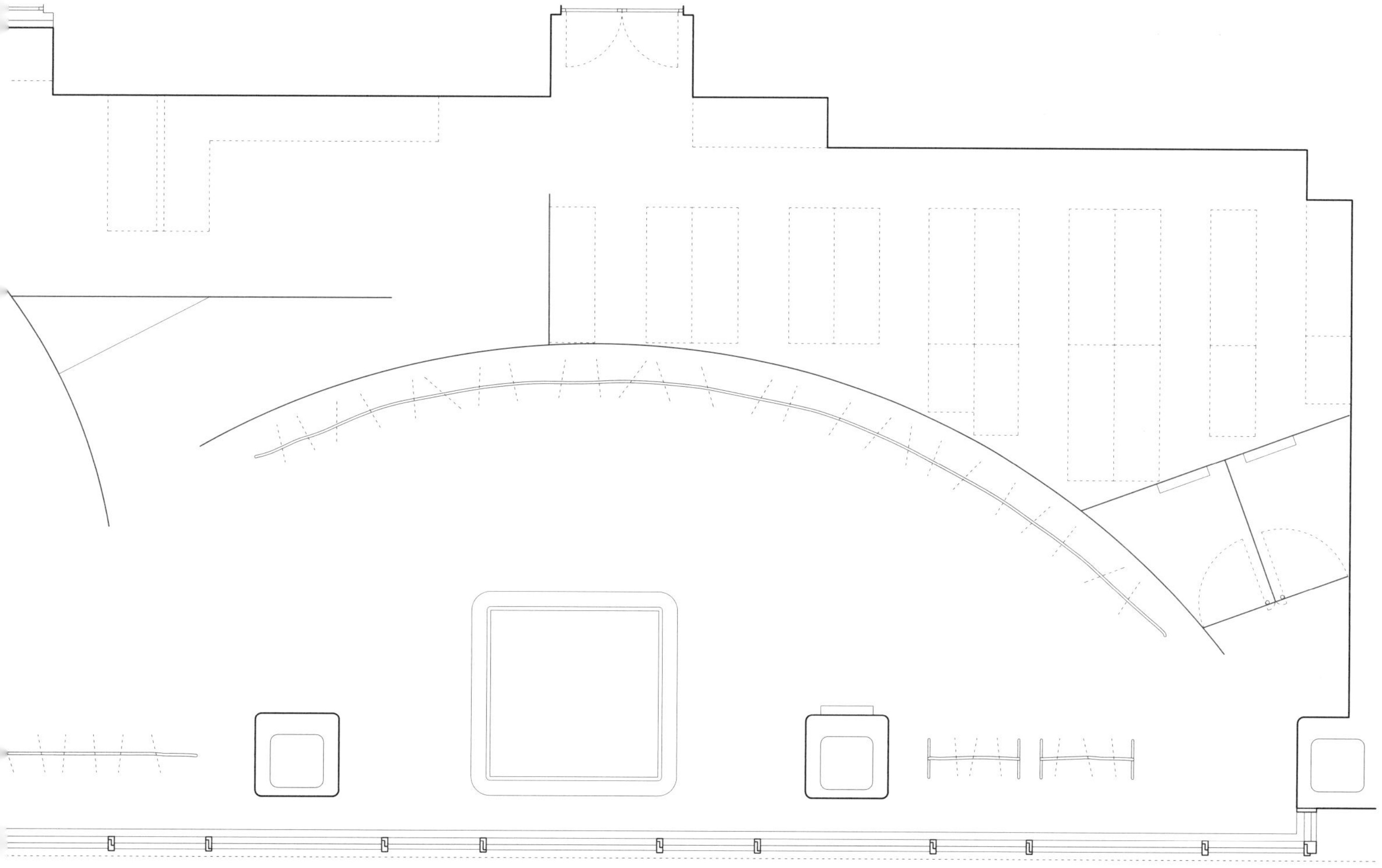

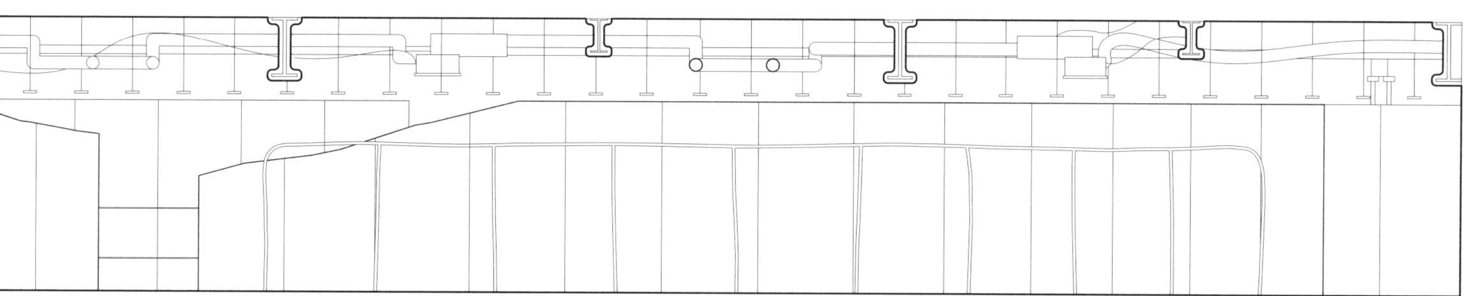

Acne Studios, Stockholm

2019-2020

This store occupies the old office space of Stockholm's former Credit Bank. On 13th August 1973, there was an attempted armed robbery in this building, and hostages were taken. Later, some of these hostages declared that they felt safer with their captor than with the police officers who were trying to rescue them. The hostages' unexpected reaction gave rise to the term "Stockholm syndrome".

Almost fifty years after that event, the building is now listed as a site of cultural heritage. The store space features neoclassical architecture, with Doric columns and marble flooring, and is divided into three rooms, organised around two central axes. This interior already had several superimposed layers, corresponding to the various renovation works that had been carried out over the previous decades, successively covering up its original state. Initial exploratory work showed that the columns and friezes were made of scagliola plaster, painted to look like marble, while the real marble flooring was in a somewhat inconsistent state of repair. After stripping away all the superfluous interventions (i.e. those not belonging to the original space), a continuous shell was made: this entailed restoring the damaged elements and plastering over other surfaces, thus creating a uniform ambience free from obstacles. Meanwhile, at the far end of the store's main area, a new marble colonnade was built; it created a kind of fake wall, like a theatrical backdrop, in order to hide the fitting rooms. This new false colonnade is made of real marble, while the existing columns are fake marble. In fact, the Ekeberg marble of the columns was extracted from the same quarry as both the original marble floor and the new marble furniture pieces, designed by Max Lamb, that accompany the store axes.

Acne Studios

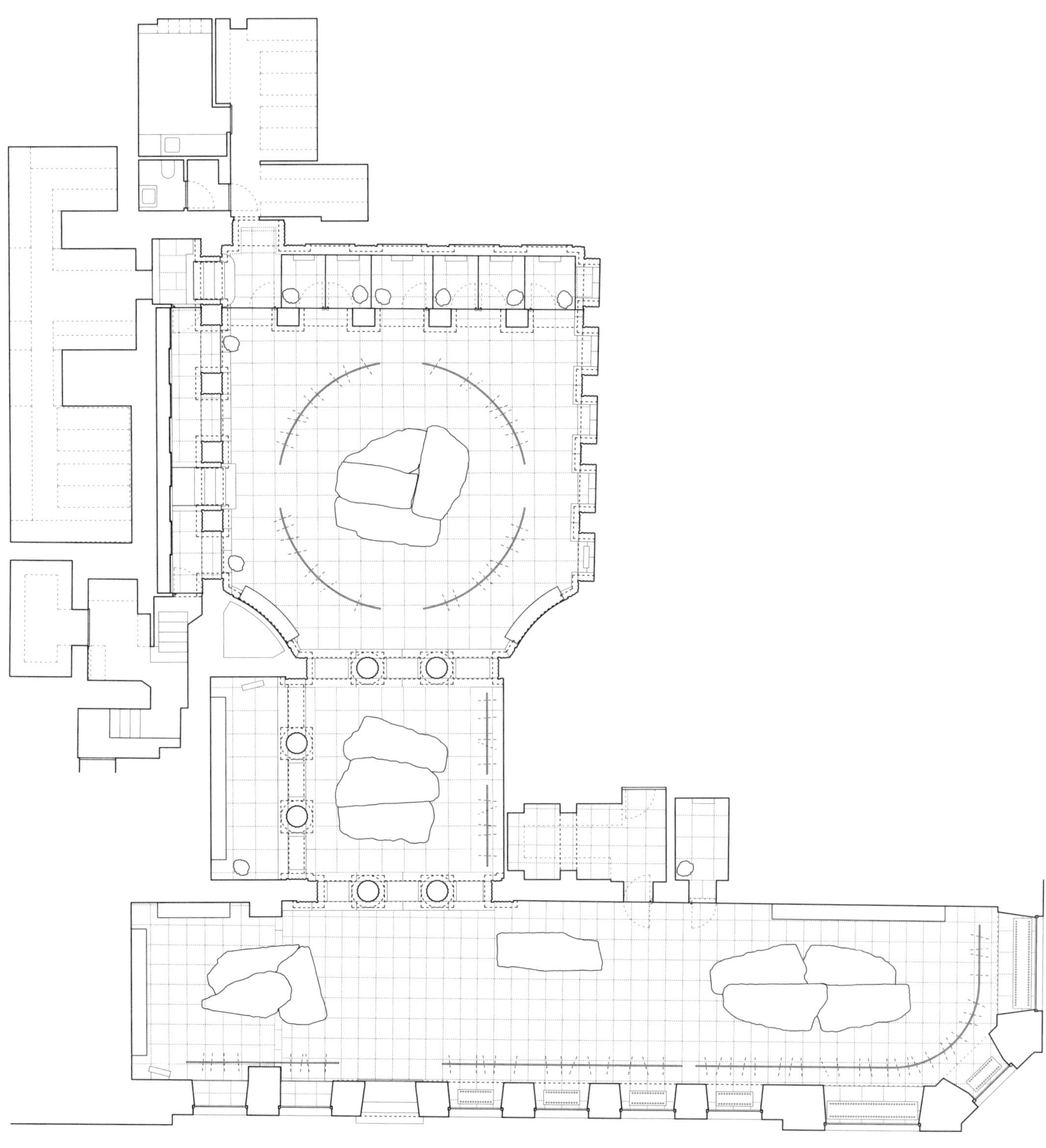

Acne Studios, Stockholm

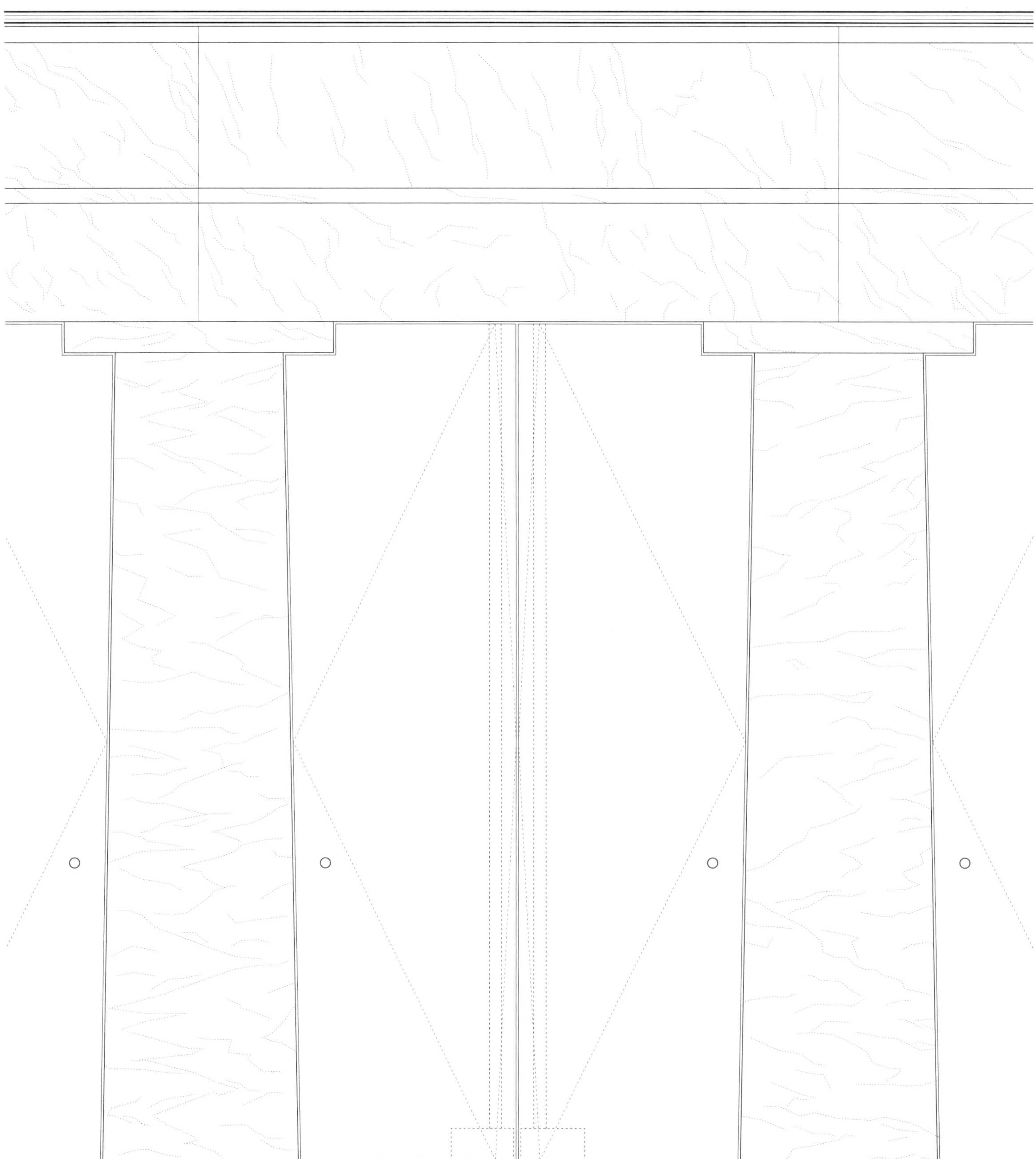

Llacuna Residential Building, Barcelona

2017-2021

This building, in the Poblenou district of Barcelona, has seven flats and two commercial premises. The building core contains the staircase, lift shaft and services, and is positioned at the centre of an irregular-shaped plot. This layout frees up the perimeter space, meaning there can be two flats on each floor that each have ventilation from two façades. On the attic level, where there is just one penthouse flat, the circular geometry of the spiral staircase is revealed in its entirety, and the living space is articulated around it.

The central staircase looks out onto the street, and also, at its highest point, onto the sky. It thus offers a range of different perspectives of the city, which change as you head upwards, and this design brings natural light and ventilation to the shared spaces.

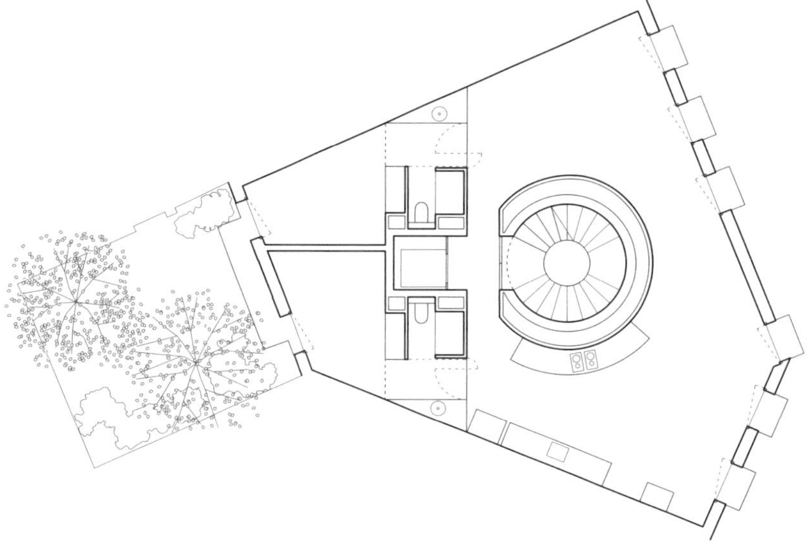

Fourth floor

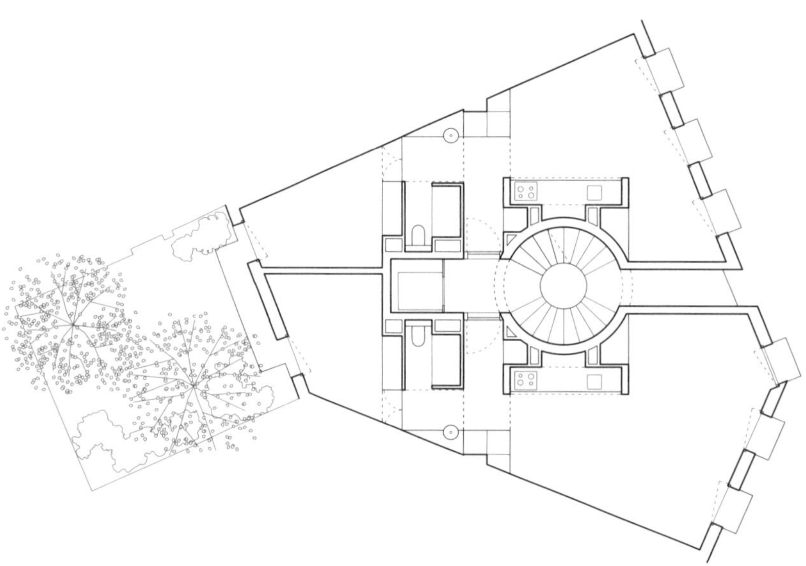

Typical floorplan

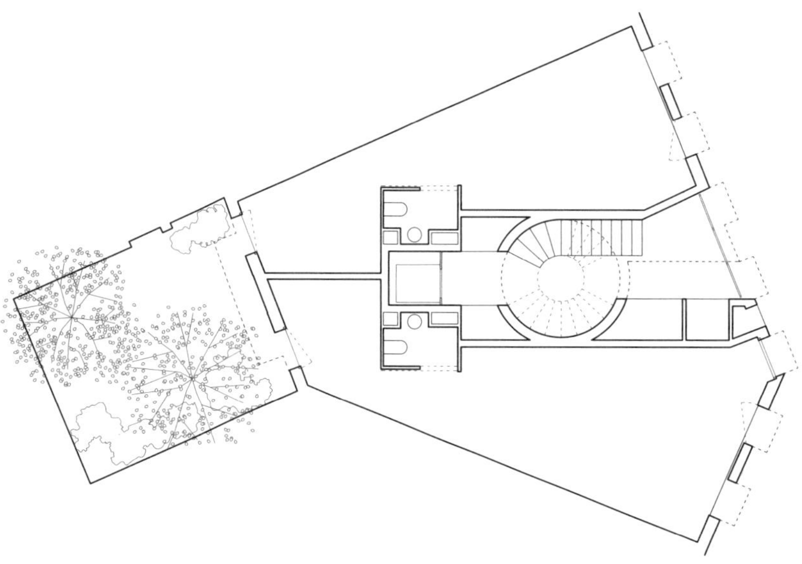

Ground floor

Acne Studios, New York

2020-2021

This store is located on the corner of an industrial building with a cast-iron structure, very typical of New York's SoHo district. The interior space has high ceilings, and is very much open to the outside. The project is resolved through a set of large triangles, in translucent glass, which contain the fitting rooms and define the store's layout and walkways. The whole space is bathed in a light hue of emerald green, creating a subtle interplay of translucent layers. This aesthetic is completed by the hazy silhouettes of people as they move around in the spaces between the panels. Just like Kate Moss in a sheer dress, at a party. Her confidence and sensuality makes everyone else look overdressed, and somewhat awkward.

These thin, 20-millimetre glass panels create a mineral landscape of rock-hard forms, contrasting greatly with the large carpeted floor upon which they stand.

© David Benett/Hulton Archive/Getty Images

ONE WAY
GRAND ST
GREENE ST
Acne Studios

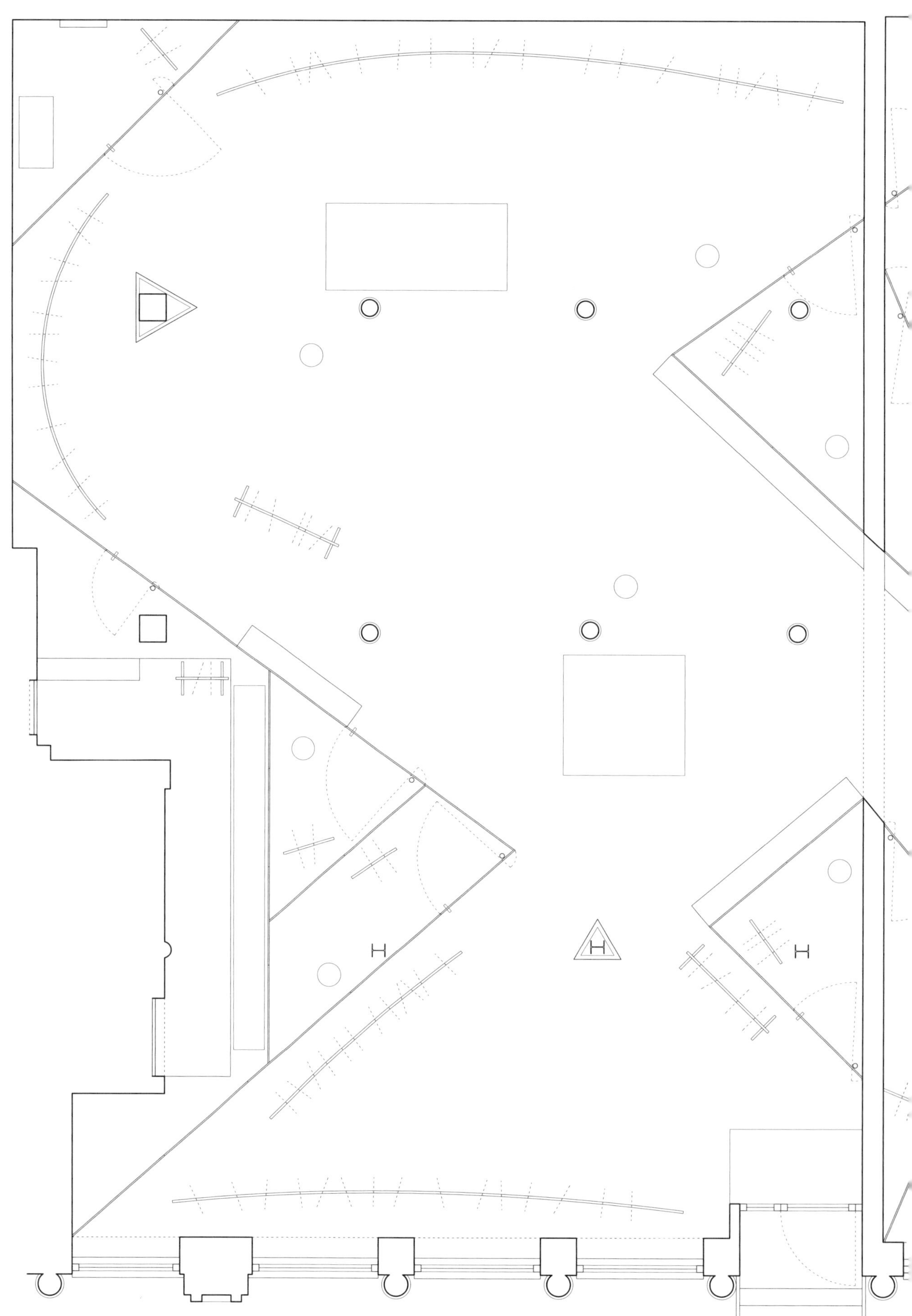

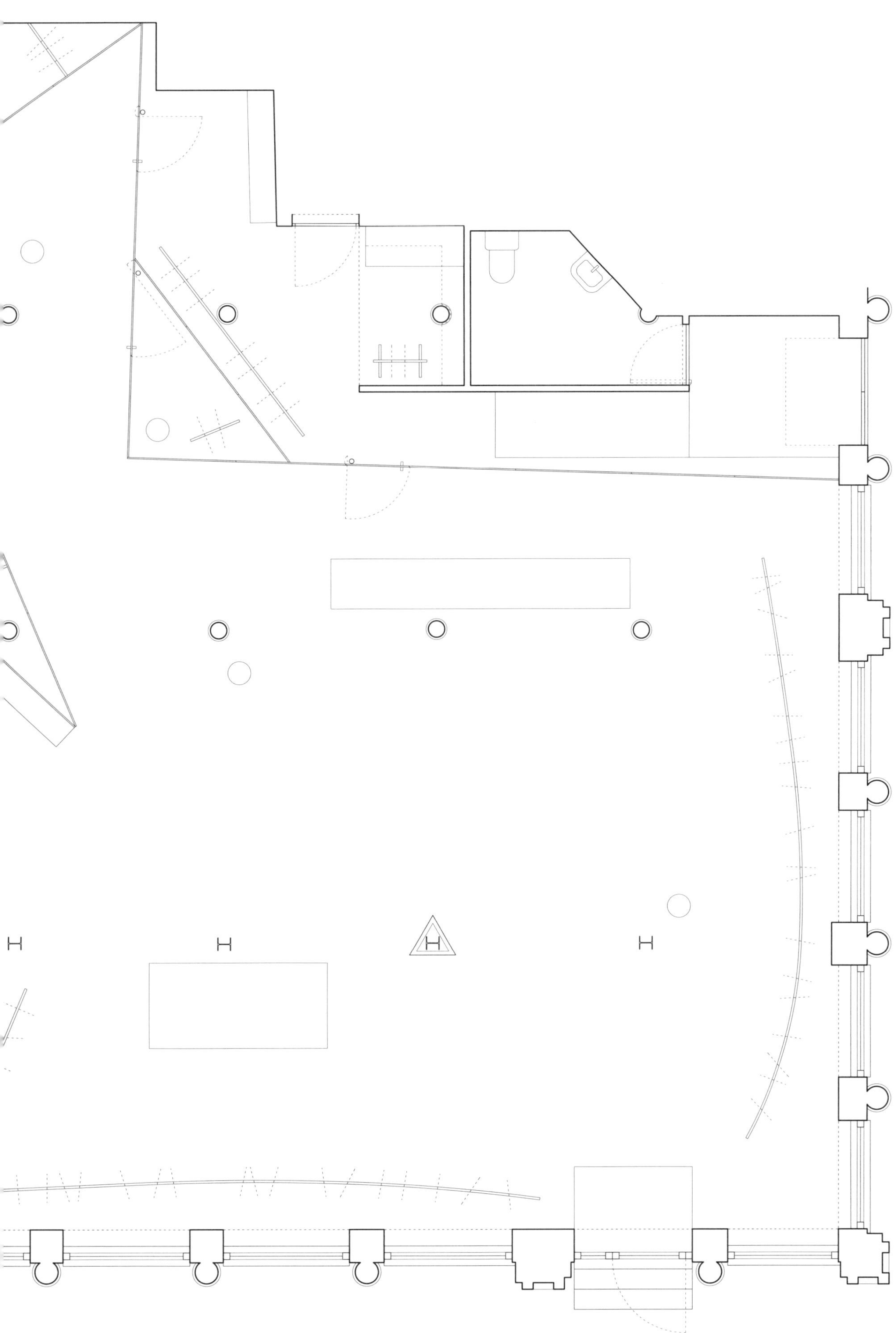

Acne Studios, New York

Acne Studios, Paris

2021-2022

This branch of Acne Studios is located on Rue Saint-Honoré, in the lower part of a corner building. Inside, it has the typical structure of an artisan's workshop-house: the ground floor has reasonably high ceilings, while there is also a mezzanine-type space with the minimum ceiling height of 2.05 metres, where the family lived. Previously, the two floors were connected by a single staircase.

As a strategic decision, the intermediate floor structure was partially demolished, thereby creating a large opening that runs the length of the store. It eventually leads to the staircase that joins the two floors, and it frees up both of them; the mezzanine ceiling thus becomes the whole store's ceiling. Also, the project seeks to forge a certain material continuity with the rest of the city: the Saint-Maximin stone used here, from a nearby quarry, is ubiquitous in Paris, and it has been used for everything from unremarkable residential buildings to the city's most iconic monuments. The store's façade was also covered with this stone, and it extends into the shop and creates a bold monolithic ambience, since all the space is constructed in this one single material. The columns next to the new overhead opening are now two floors high, and they loom over the space almost like imposing urban infrastructure. The floor-to-ceiling windows, simple panes of glass slotted between the interior and exterior stonework, open the store out and into the city, thus sparking up a dialogue between the two.

Detail of a cutwater on Pont Neuf, Paris, in Saint-Maximin stone.

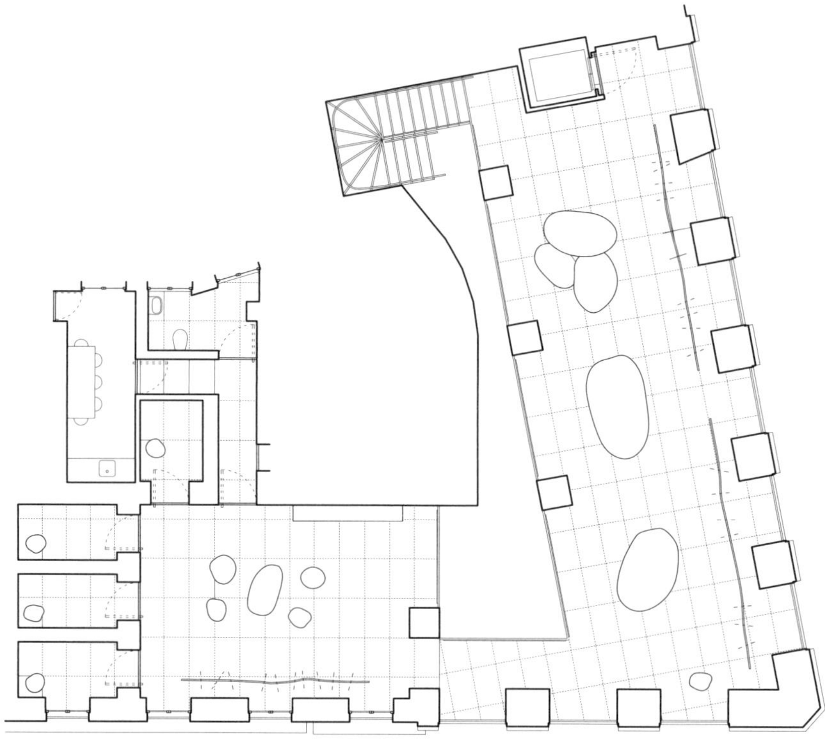

Mezzanine

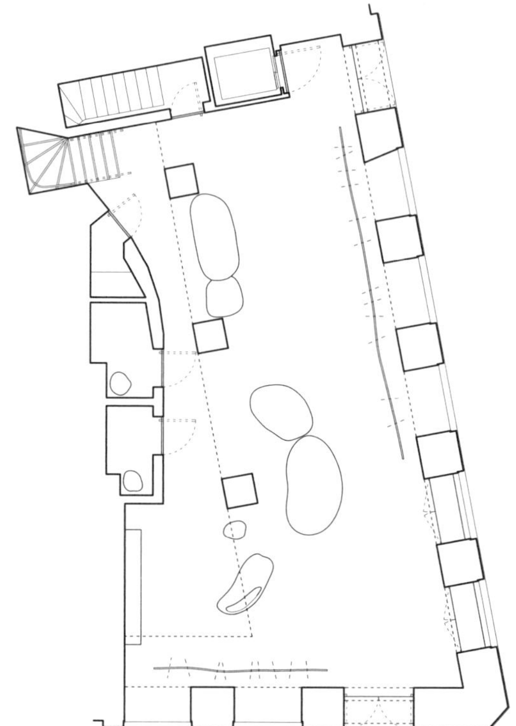

Ground floor

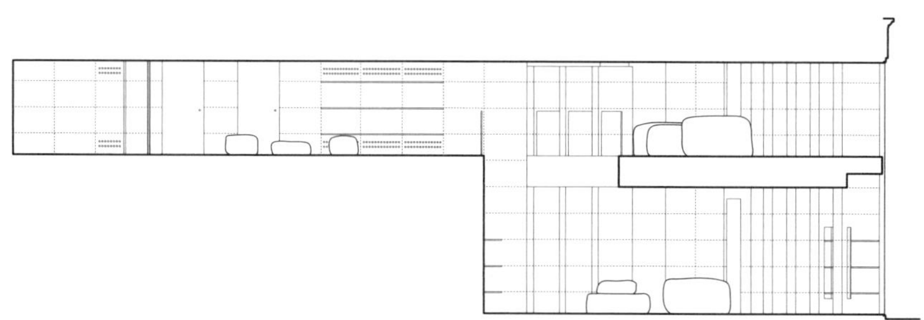

Royal St-Honoré
Royal St-Honoré
Royal St-Honoré
Christofle
Christofle
PARIS
Acne Studios
Acne Studios

Praga Residential Building, Barcelona

2019-2021

A teacher of ours once spoke about how fascinating skin is. He focused on the mouth, lips and nose, noting how the skin goes inside the body (without ceasing to be skin) and then, at some indeterminate point, it turns from something exterior into something interior.

This residential building, containing a pair of duplex apartments and four other flats, is located on a very steep street, on a plot between party walls. Most buildings like this are resolved by making a compact block with one main façade, and another façade at the back. Ideally, the rear façade looks onto a patio, but, in the worst-case scenario, just the bare-minimum, legally required gap is left instead, in order to provide some degree of ventilation to the far end of the plot. This project aims to break with the idea of main and rear façades, by building just one: from the street, the façade folds in on itself, towards the inside of the plot, thus forming a more urban-type patio rather than the usual domestic one. All of the flats and shared spaces overlook this patio, without losing sight of the street.

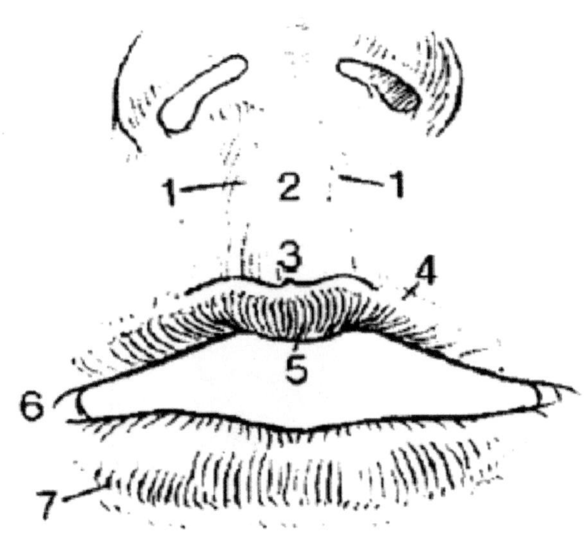

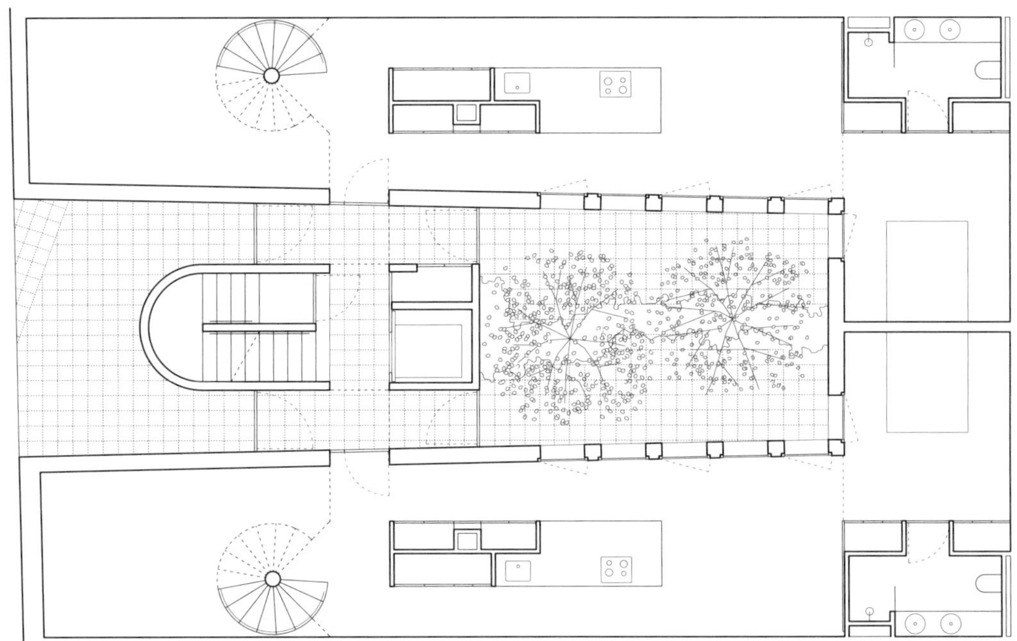

Ground floor

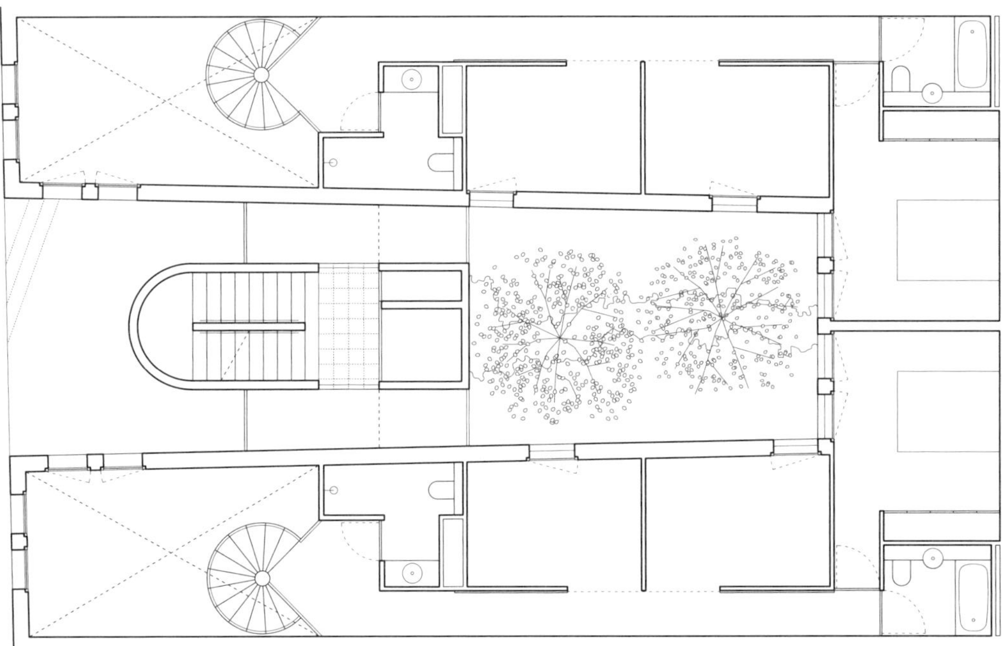

First floor

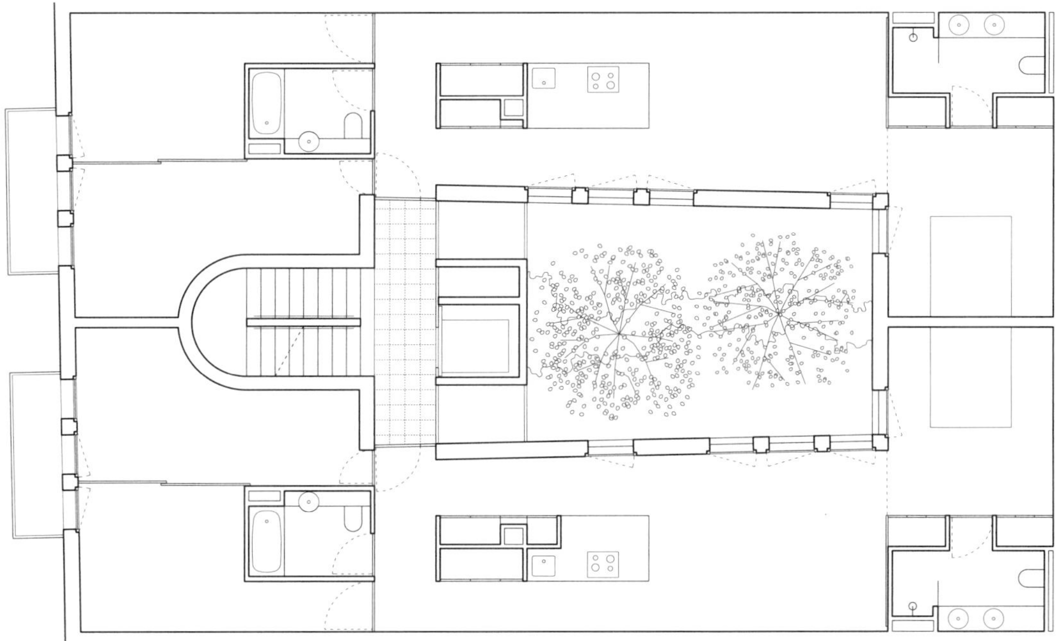

Typical floorplan

Longitudinal section

Verdi House, Barcelona

2018-2021

This house is located in the upper area of Barcelona's Gràcia district. It is one in a row of small houses, each of which look onto a back garden that is on a lower level than the entrance area. These houses, built in the early 20th century, are not particularly noteworthy, apart from their façades which now have protected status.

Behind Verdi House's façade, which acts as a kind of mask, the space gradually steps down to the garden by means of a series of half-floors that are also gardens themselves. The floor structure covers the span between the party walls, without the need for columns: this way, all levels are totally open, from the front façade to the rear. These half-floors find their breaking-point in the area under the skylight, where the staircase and circulation spaces are located.

To offer some protection from the sun, the house is covered in wooden shutters. Their slats ensure that the indoor space sits in half-light, while retaining its openness. The proportion of these slats, and the full/empty rhythm they bring to the space, is the same as in Barcelona's "Umbráculo", the shaded pavilion built in 1883-1884 by Josep Fontseré i Mestre.

Verdi House, Barcelona

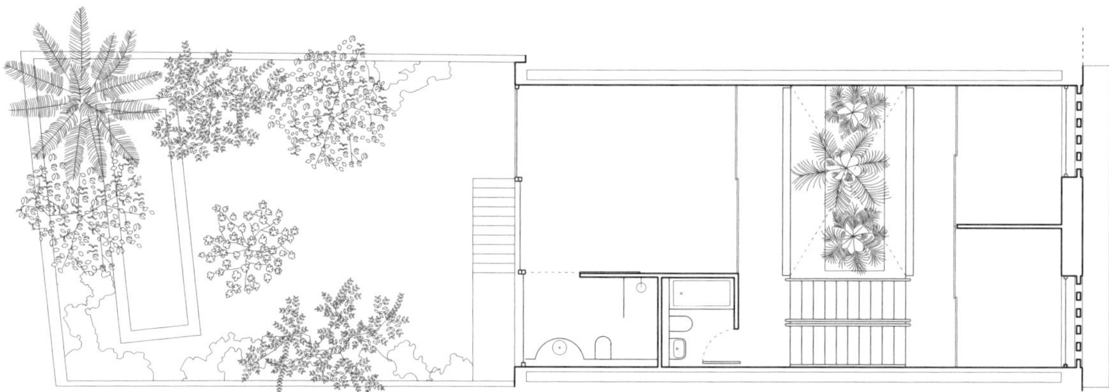

First floor

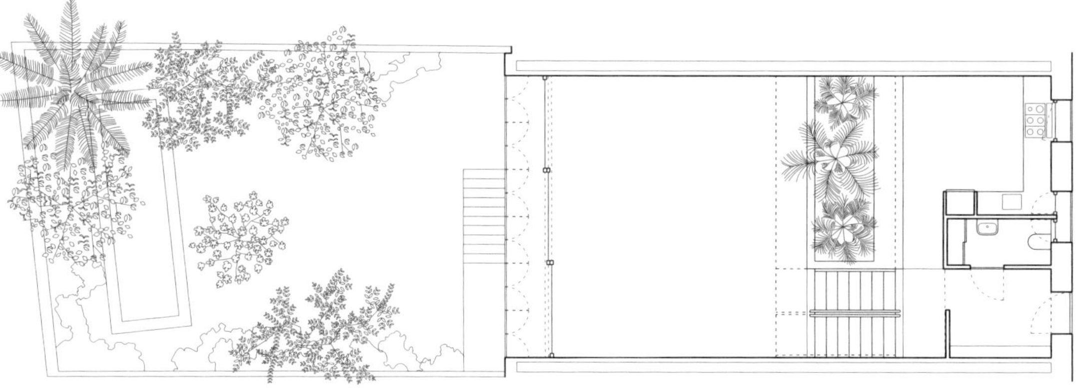

Ground floor

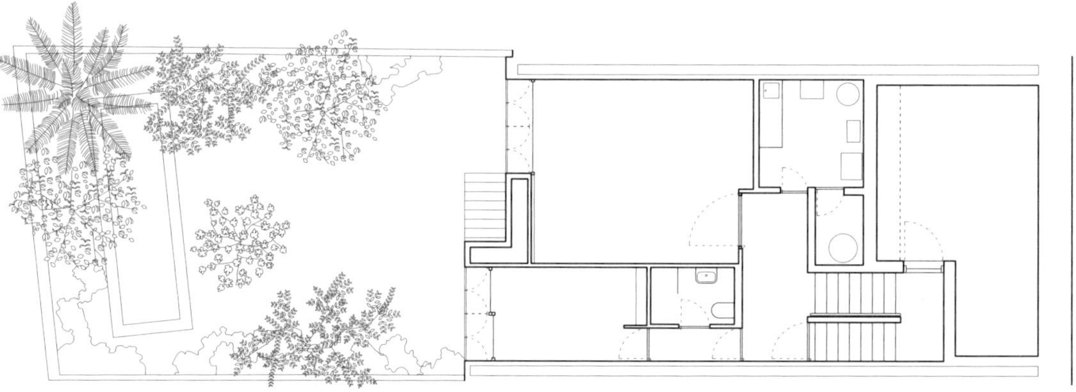

Basement

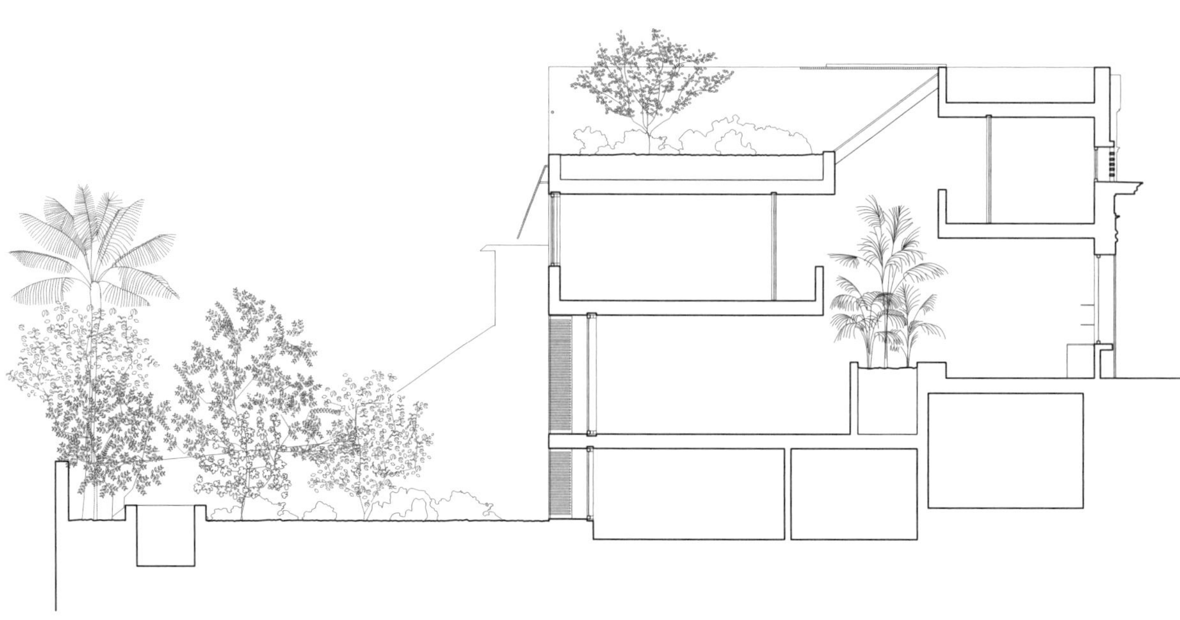

Verdi House, Barcelona

Verdi House, Barcelona

Costa House, Barcelona

2019-2021

Costa House sits on an elongated plot between party walls, in a quiet Barcelona neighbourhood. It has three floors overlooking a garden, with a column running through them, and a staircase. As a result, the house feels like a habitable porch which spills out into the garden, with floor-to-ceiling sliding windows that allow the building to be completely opened to the outdoors. Several birch trees and a curtain silently control the sunlight, all fluttering in the breeze. The main façade is understood as just another perimeter wall, concealing a house which, as in the 1892 painting by Ramon Casas, is an *Open-Air Interior*. Casas painted this particular part of his house on numerous occasions; it is neither indoors nor outdoors, a sheltered space, yet out in the fresh air.

43
LOCAL EN

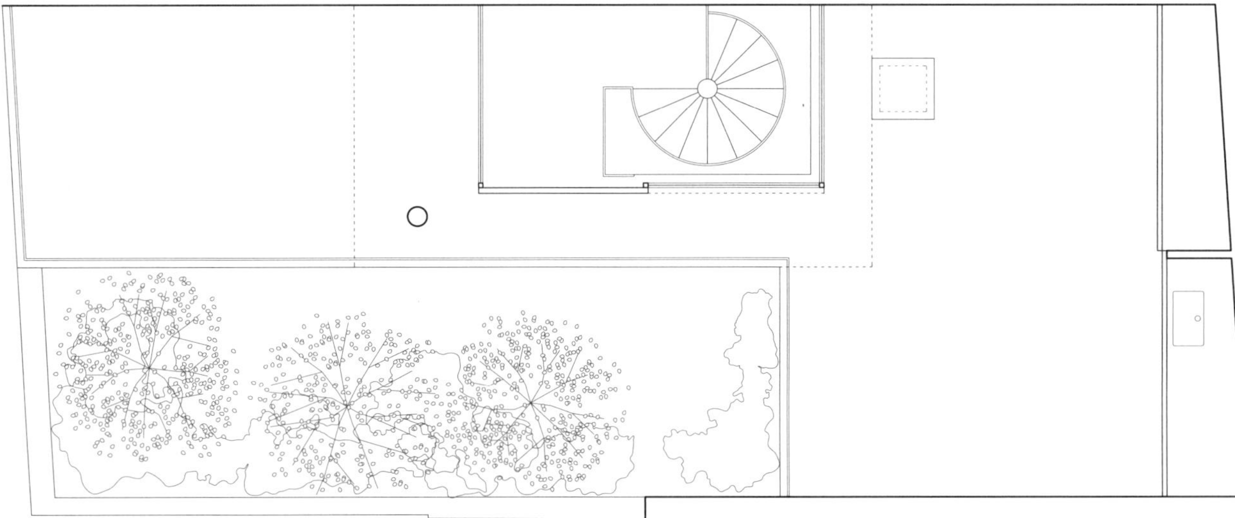

Second floor

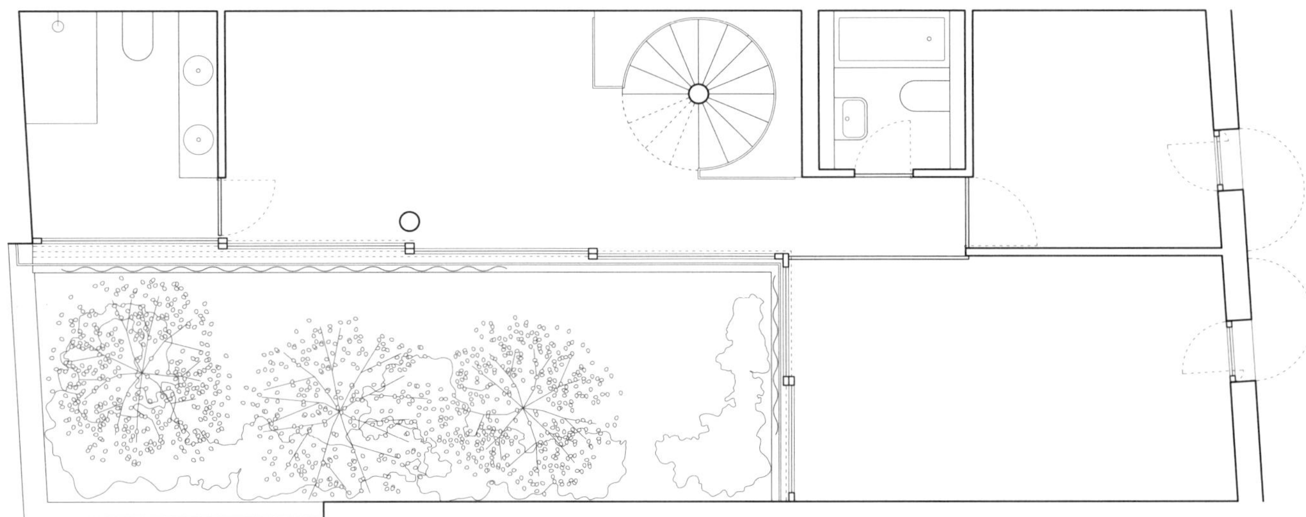

First floor

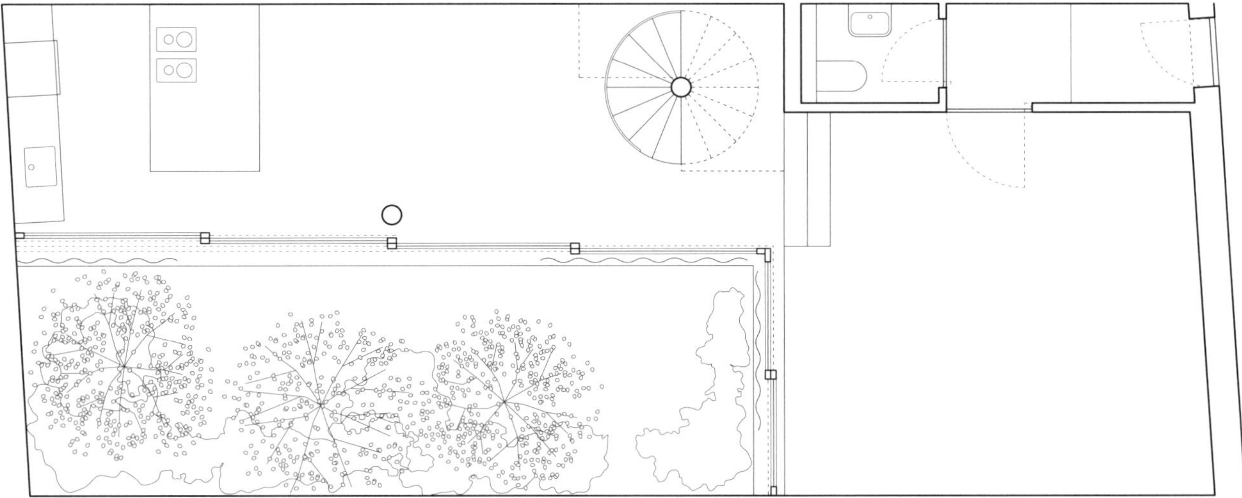

Ground floor

Costa House, Barcelona

Costa House, Barcelona

Quinta da Ponte, Sintra

2019-

This project is an intervention on a *quinta de recreio* in Sintra, near Lisbon. *Quintas de recreio* are a kind of agricultural estate which is now dying out: they have an area of self-sufficient land, with woodland, vegetable gardens, fruit trees, livestock and buildings, but they are not farms per se. They combine, in one space, agricultural production and bourgeois residence, which overlap and complement each other. In the past, the production areas would be dotted with tiled architectural elements, often related with water: these buildings would serve as areas for rest and recreation, as well as providing hydraulic or agricultural infrastructure. The romantic paths on these estates, alongside meticulously-planted rows of trees and flowers, would follow the irrigation channels flowing from the tanks; those walking by would hear water babbling away. Windmills, with their bold verticality, would bring up water from the wells. In short, in the same time and space, disparate elements coexisted and came together: the stench of manure and the sweet smell of roses climbing the trellises, drinking water and irrigation water, crop planning and literary debates, fruit trees and shaded areas for relaxing in, the productive and the decorative, food for the body and food for the soul.

Our project revives a *quinta de recreio* that had been abandoned for decades. This particular one has a manor house and a formal garden, as well as some auxiliary outbuildings and a handful of other elements that we gradually uncovered behind all the vegetation: windmills, decorated water tanks, a dovecote, fountains and pergolas. We also came across an array of mines and wells that would funnel the undersoil water into a complex hydraulic system that follows the lay of the land, arranged around one north-south axis, and another east-west one. There are also the remains of grapevines on the southern side of the plot, and woodland on its northern edge. The flat areas of land had fruit, cereal and vegetable crops in the better-irrigated parts.

The client is an art collector, who told us of his desire to get this *quinta* up and running again, remaining faithful to its original spirit. Several buildings are to be restored, and new ones are being built. The landscape and production areas are being restructured in up-to-date ways, with a keen focus on respecting biodiversity.

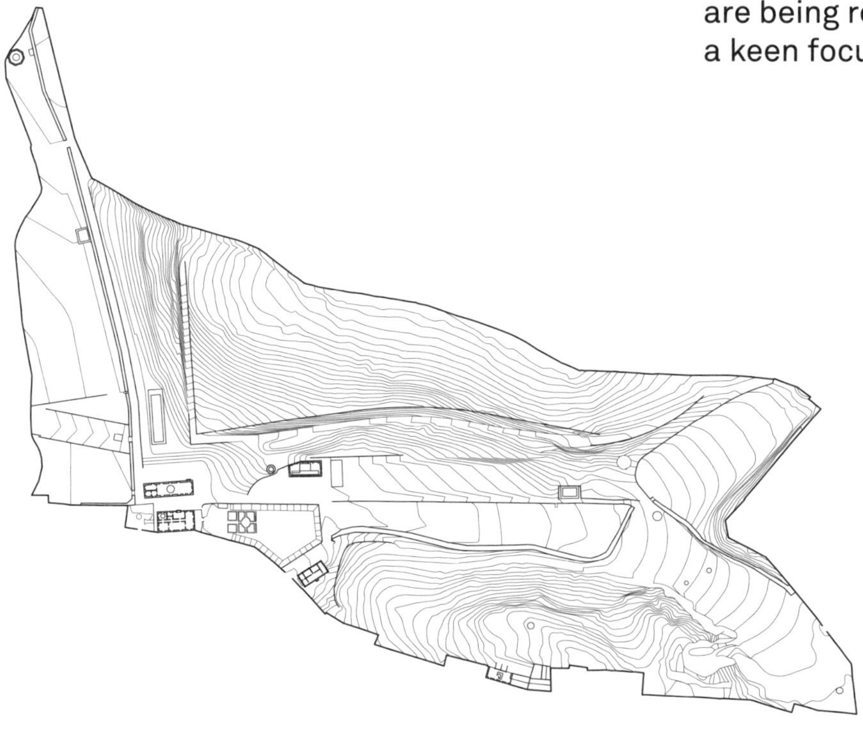

Tenant House, Sintra

2020-2022

This was the first building to be transformed at the Quinta da Ponte complex. It is part of a row of buildings along the perimeter wall of the estate, and their sunken ground floor spaces, having been excavated in the terrain, were previously small shops that only opened onto the main façade. This building's upper floor, which could not be accessed from the one below, was a single-floor apartment mostly cut off from the estate.

The aim of this project was to invert the building's original function—both in terms of the interior space and its relation with the exterior—yet without changing the volume, in order to preserve the row's uniformity. The main façade looks onto a narrow street with an even narrower pavement, with traffic going by. This façade is now reformulated as the rear one, in an attempt to open up the building onto the estate instead, both visually and with regards to its function. The upper floor has four large window bays, two of which also reach down to the ground floor, forming two patios. This means that the bedrooms can be moved downstairs, along with the wet rooms; thus, the main upper floor, which is now completely freed up, becomes a large shared space with a connection to the estate. In turn, it is presided over by a staircase crowned by the kitchen that articulates the space.

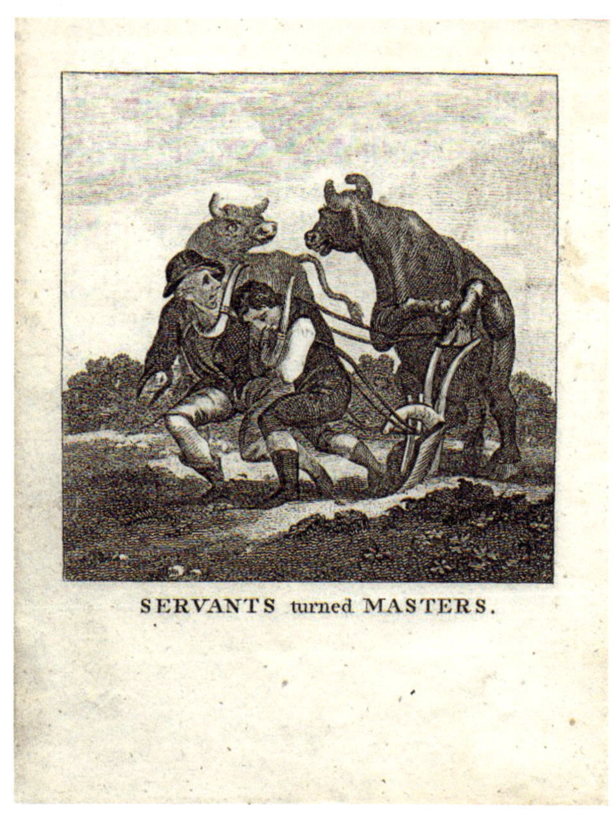

Jean and Ann Taylor, *World Turned Upside-Down*, 1810.

First floor

Ground floor

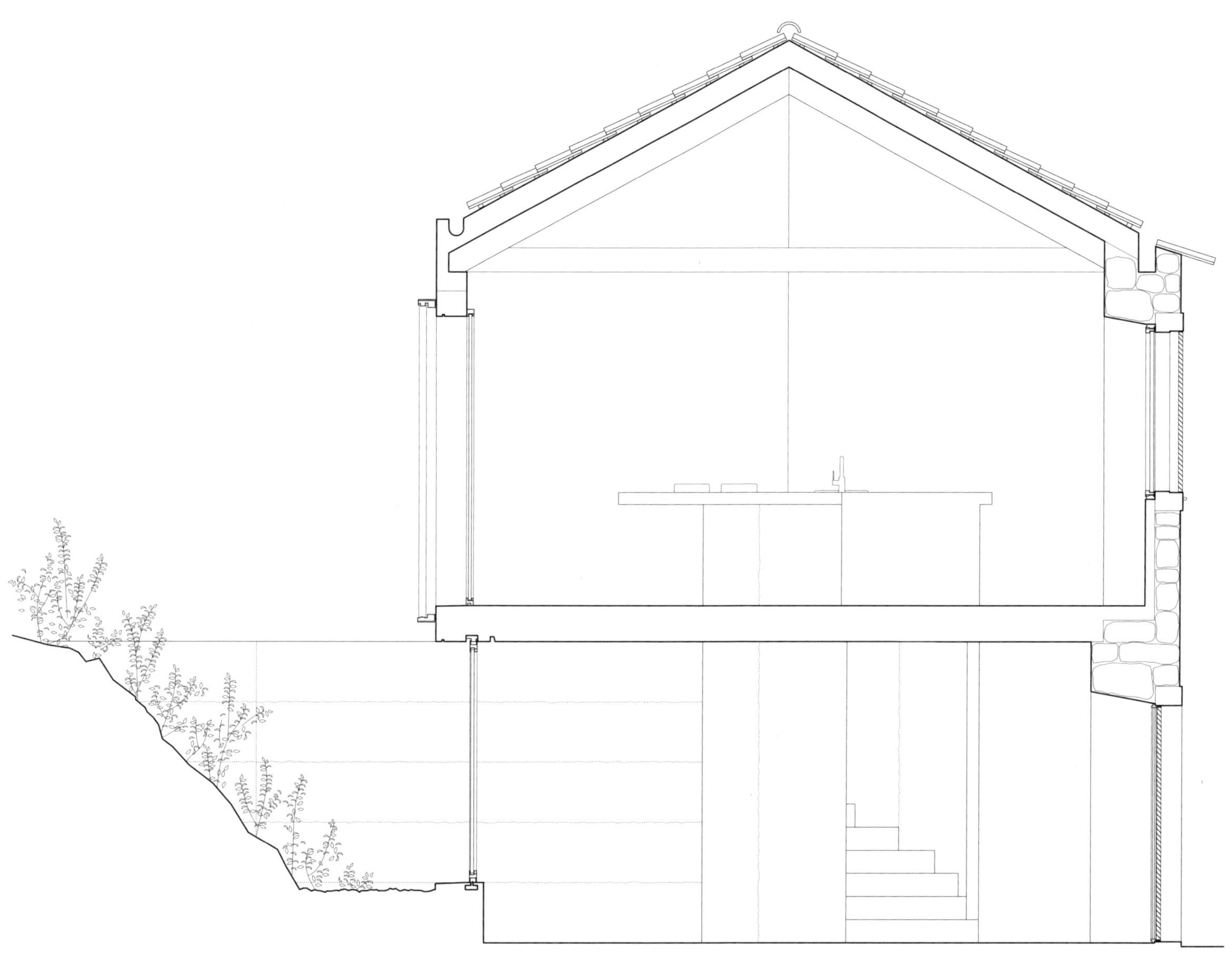

Garage and Groundskeeper's House, Sintra

2021-

This small building will replace an old auxiliary outbuilding on the estate, one which has deteriorated beyond repair. The new project's maximum floor plan, main volumetric features and roof material (ceramic tiles) must be the same as in the original structure due to regulations. The design also includes certain signature elements that are related to the architectural language of other pieces on the estate, as seen in the chimney or the proportion of some of the windows.

The building is located next to the complex's main entrance for vehicles, and it will serve as a garage space and a residence for the estate's groundskeeper. The lay of the land means that the building can have two distinct faces, on its two respective floors; on the ground floor, the garage doors open completely onto the entrance road, while up on the first floor the apartment looks out onto the opposite side, with views of the vineyards and a south-facing orientation. There is no internal connection between both floors —they work as two separate elements under the same roof.

The existing building was constructed right up against another one, which does not currently belong to the estate. The new project, however, is detached from the other building, and a walkway goes between the two: this way, it stands free as an independent piece in its own right, among the estate's constellation of architectures.

Janus, Roman god, protector of the state and guardian of doorways and gates. His two faces look forwards and back, one to the future and one to the past.

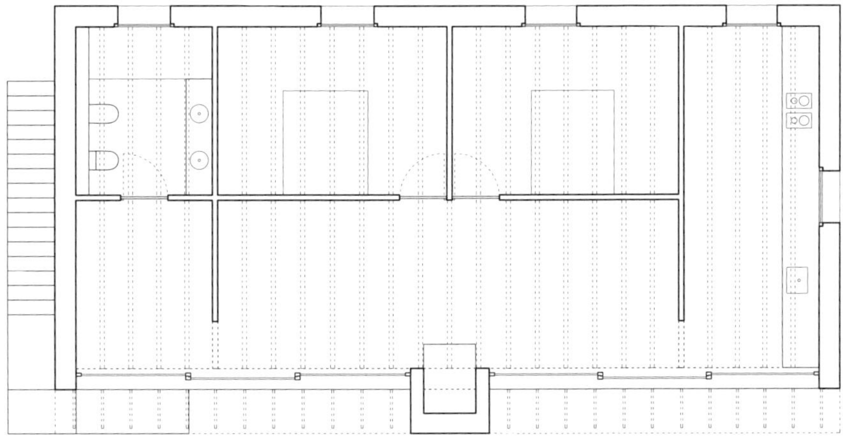

Fisrt floor

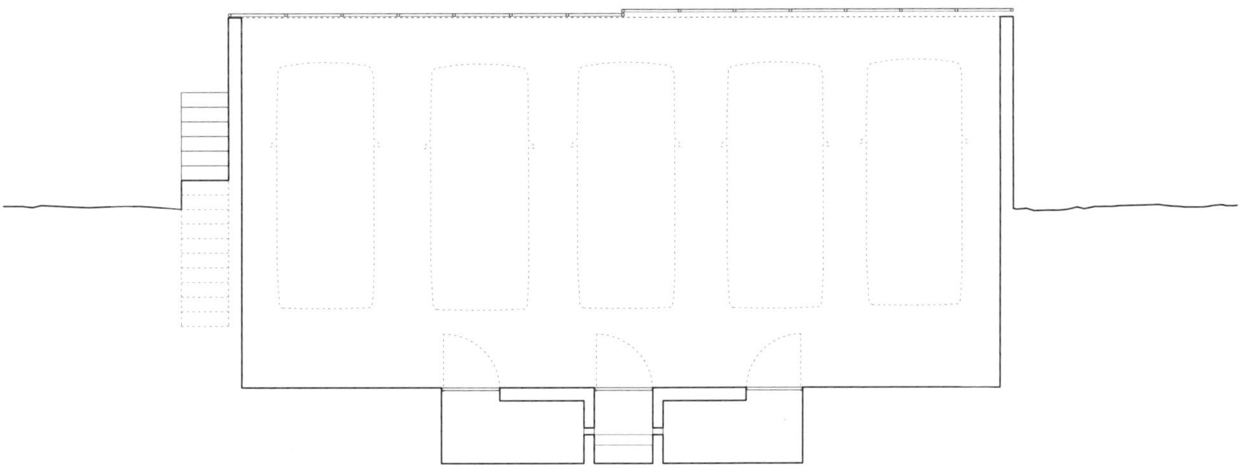

Ground floor

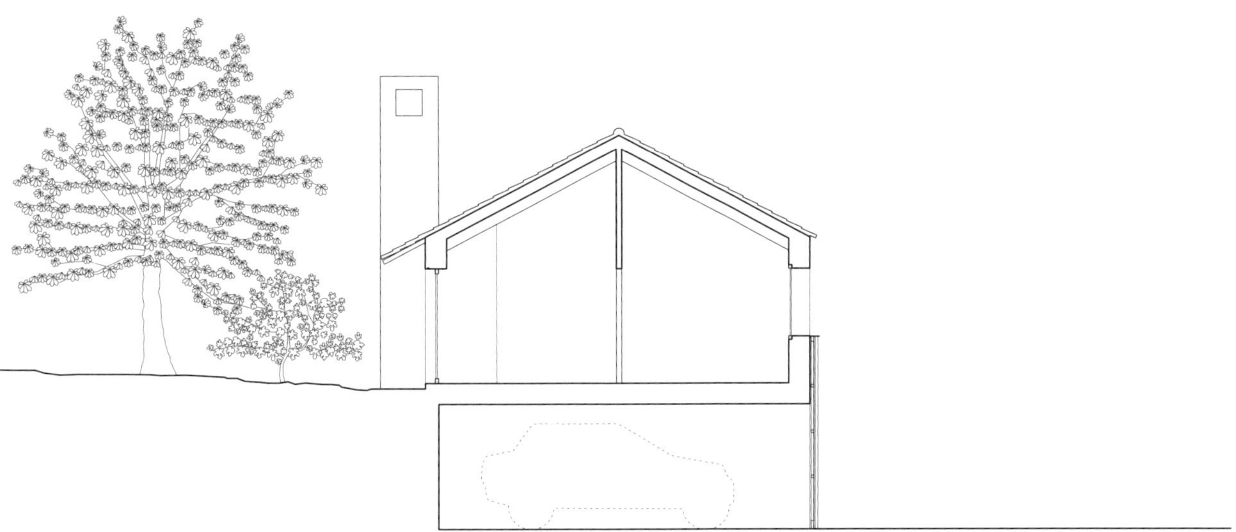

Patio House, Aiguablava

2021-

Located on a terrain that slopes down towards the sea, the house's living space sits beneath a roof/porch that follows the shape of the plot. As a habitable perimeter, the roof traces a complete ring around the house, as well as two patios demarcated by a colonnade. The main patio, measuring 15 × 15 metres, has a pond and three trees for shade, while the smaller patio serves as the entrance. The sliding doors onto the patio can be opened completely, leaving the rooms exposed to the outside, while also revealing the house's structure. Slatted shutters provide shade from the sun, while also allowing the breeze to run through.

The house's rooms all fit within the variable-width porch/roof space, which turns into a corridor and shared spaces as you walk through the patios. The Egyptian gardens, which are symmetrical, geometric and rigid, are organised around a pond, with its own irrigation channels and fruit trees. Similarly, in this case, another geometric pond orders and brings a sense of scale to the surrounding garden, which is both covered and in the open at different points.

Part of a fresco in the Tomb of Nebamun, Thebes (present-day Luxor), Egypt. Eighteenth Dynasty.

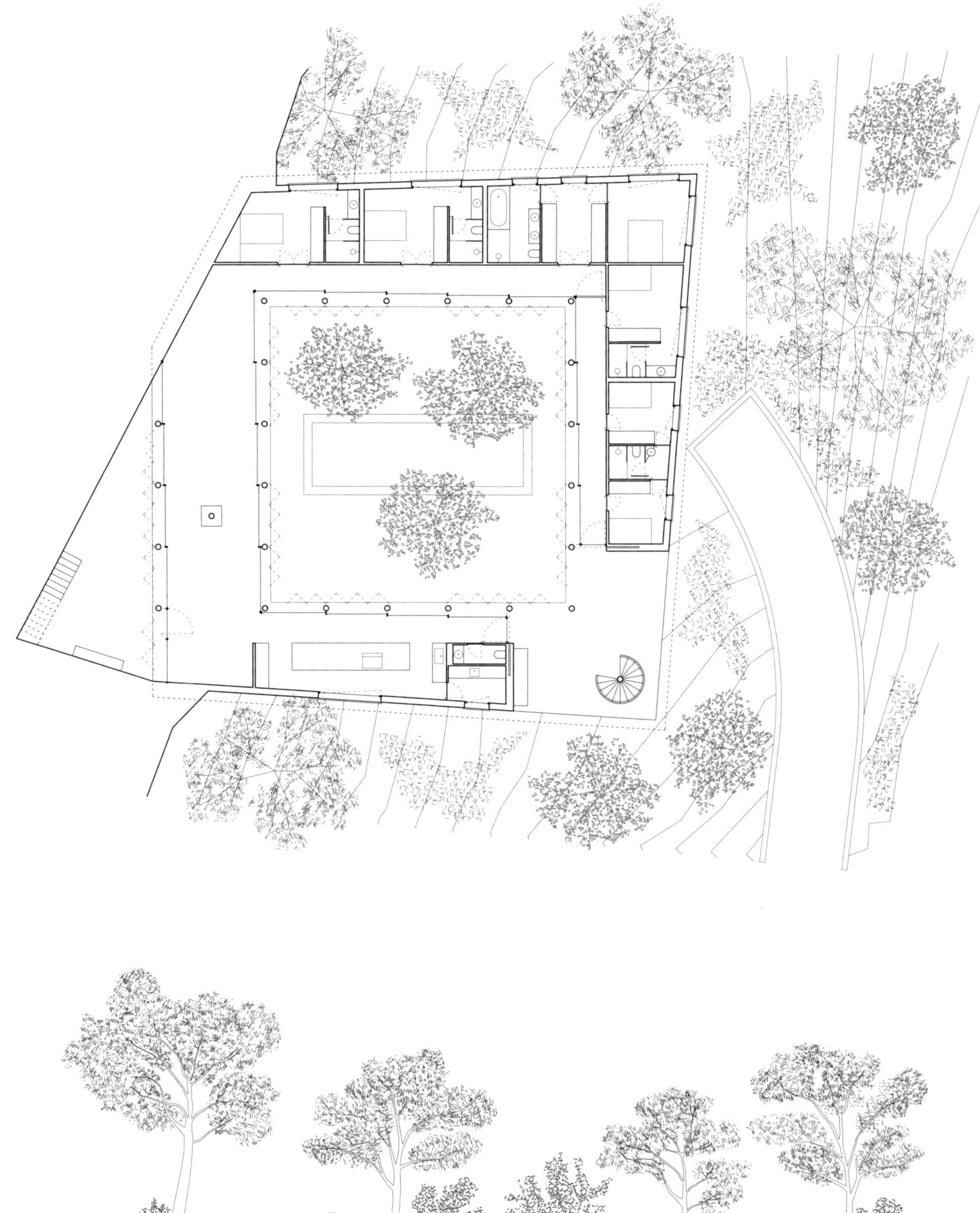

House in Collserola, Barcelona

2022-

This house is built on a very steep-sloping plot. To deal with this situation, the project features a structure over split levels, on half-floors, which means that it can have a swimming pool on the roof. A staircase crosses the house where the two distinct levels meet, dividing it in two and providing access to both parts. Floor-to-ceiling sliding windows open up the house completely, cleanly revealing the concrete structure. Rollable wooden blinds provide shade, while also letting air in.

The project proposes that only the indispensable elements be built, those you need in order to inhabit a structure. That is, the kind of things that you could almost pick up and cart somewhere else, to take over a different structure, if and when you need to move.

Water tank in Aswan, Egypt.

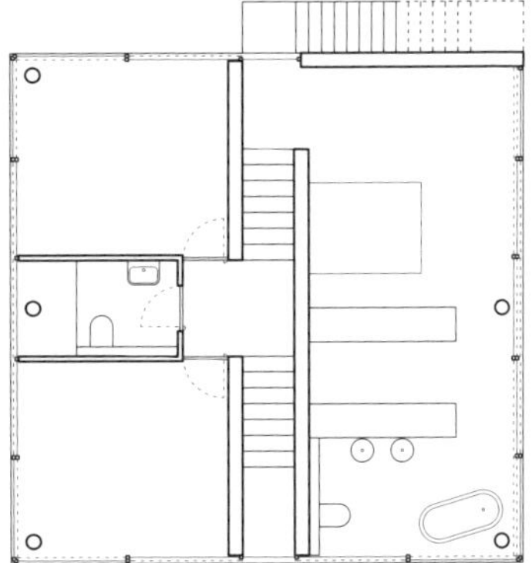

First floor

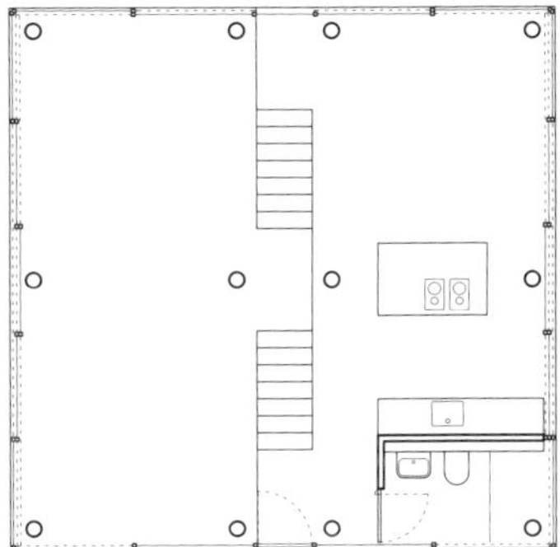

Ground floor

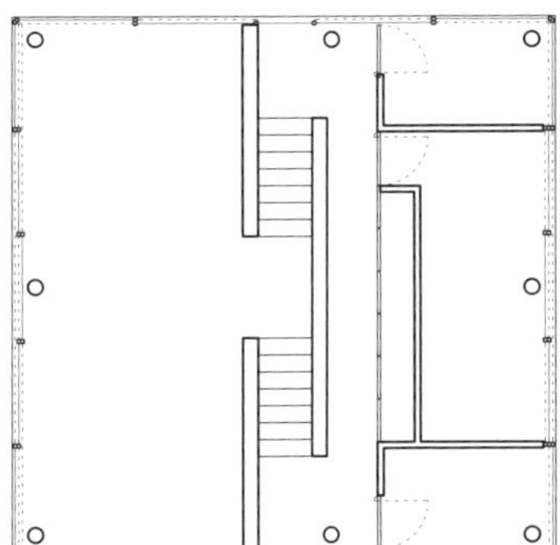

Basement

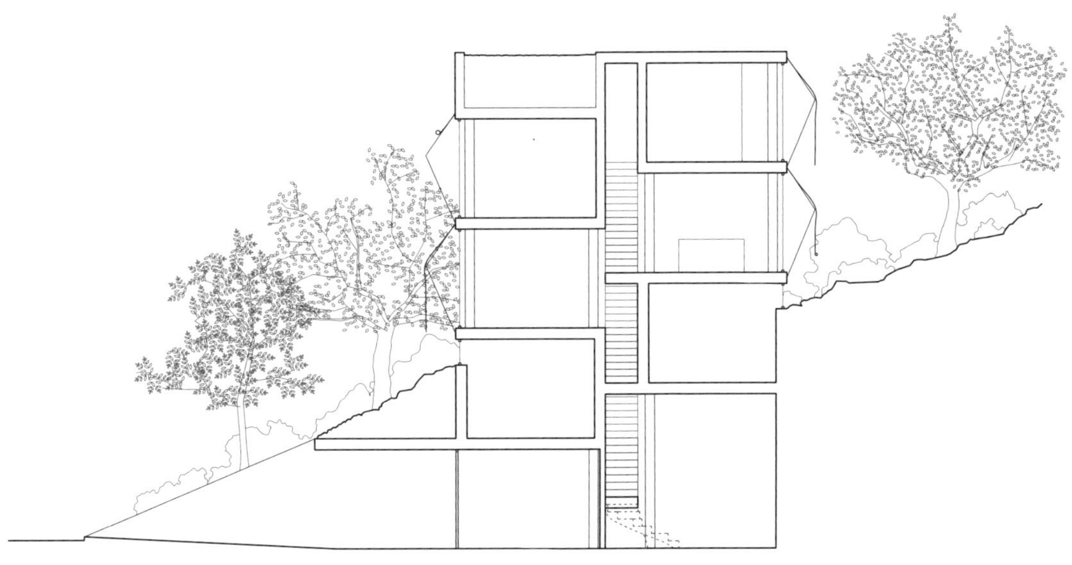

Apartamento Headquarters, Barcelona

2021-

The team at Apartamento (the publishing house and magazine of the same name) asked us to convert an old garage, located within a block in Barcelona's Eixample district, into their new head office. This unit, which is open-plan and nicely proportioned, is in a state of ruin: its fibre-cement gable roof rests upon seven wooden trusses, some of which are on the verge of collapse.

In order to make the most of Barcelona's climate, this project seeks to establish a constant connection with the outdoors. Therefore, the design features a central patio, which splits the office in two: this way, of the four spaces set out in the brief, one of them is on one side of the patio and the remaining three are on the other side. Workers must go outside and cross the patio if they need to go from one space to another.

The new exterior walls (i.e. the two new façades that look onto the patio), in simple glass, represent a fine line between the indoor space and the outdoor climate, with its changing seasons. A light auxiliary structure has a series of wooden roll-up blinds that control the solar radiation and filter the light by changing the building's envelope.

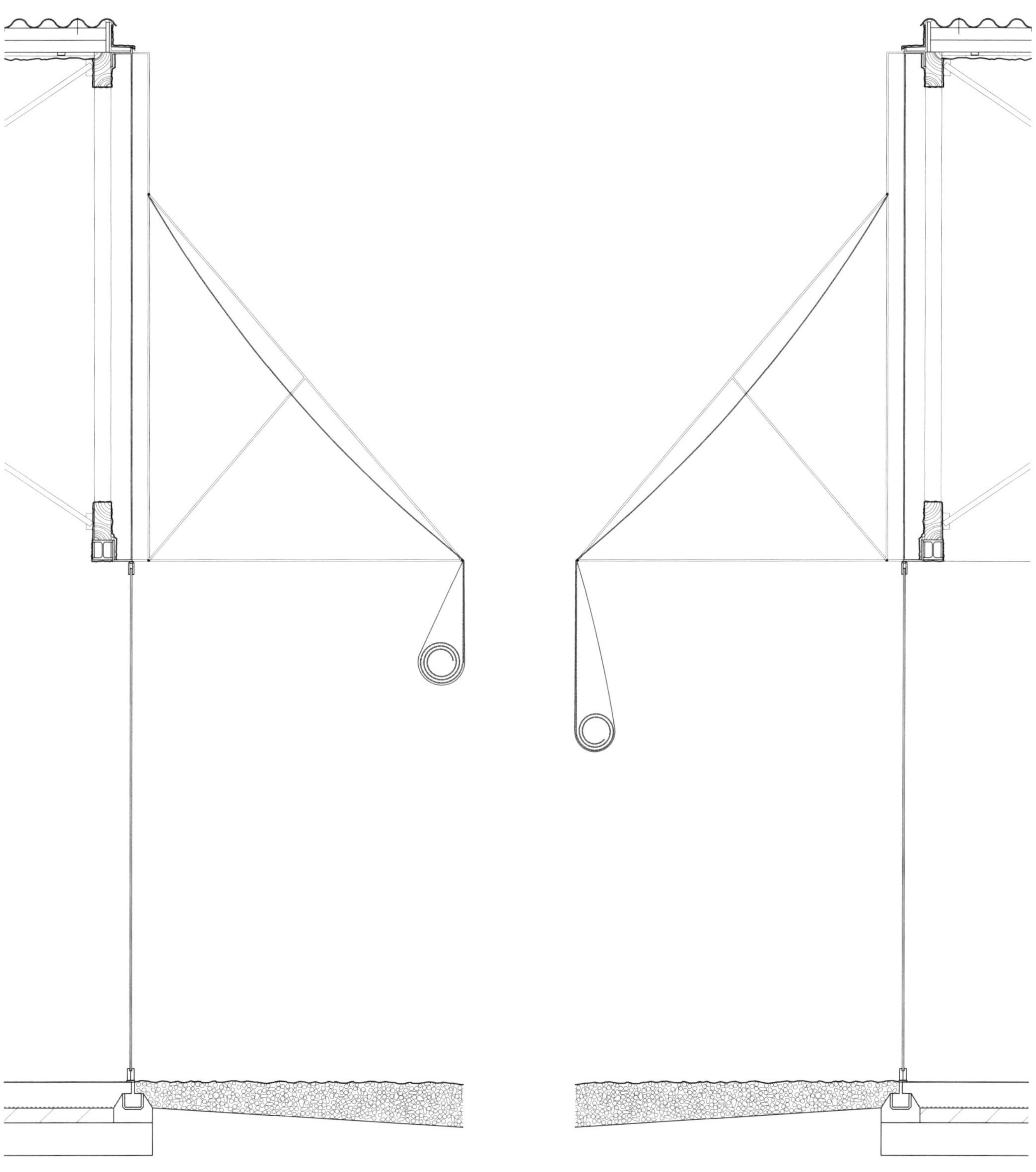

Credits

Apartment for Nacho

Location Barcelona, Spain
Design Arquitectura-G (Jonathan Arnabat, Jordi Ayala-Bril, Aitor Fuentes and Igor Urdampilleta)
Design and construction years 2011-2012
Client Nacho Alegre
Photographs José Hevia

Luz House

Location Cilleros (Cáceres), Spain
Design Arquitectura-G (Jonathan Arnabat, Jordi Ayala-Bril, Aitor Fuentes and Igor Urdampilleta)
Design and construction years 2011-2013
Client Luz Almeida
Structure engineer Ofici:Arquitectura
Photographs José Hevia

Luz House II

Location Madrid, Spain
Design Arquitectura-G (Jonathan Arnabat, Jordi Ayala-Bril, Aitor Fuentes and Igor Urdampilleta)
Project team Albert Estruga, Jaime Fernández, Albert Guerra
Design and construction years 2017-2018
Client Luz Almeida
Structure engineer Ofici:Arquitectura
MEP engineer TDI Enginyers
Photographs José Hevia

Acne Studios, Nagoya

Location Nagoya, Japan
Design Arquitectura-G (Jonathan Arnabat, Jordi Ayala-Bril, Aitor Fuentes and Igor Urdampilleta)
Project team Diogo Porto
Design and construction year 2019
Client Acne Studios
Lighting Benoit Lalloz
Photographs José Hevia

Acne Studios, Stockholm

Location Stockholm, Sweden
Design Arquitectura-G (Jonathan Arnabat, Jordi Ayala-Bril, Aitor Fuentes and Igor Urdampilleta)
Project team Diogo Porto, Elena Tarilonte
Design and construction years 2019-2020
Client Acne Studios
Lighting Benoit Lalloz
Furniture Max Lamb
Photographs José Hevia

Llacuna Residential Building

Location: Barcelona, Spain
Design Arquitectura-G (Jonathan Arnabat, Jordi Ayala-Bril, Aitor Fuentes and Igor Urdampilleta)
Project team Albert Guerra, Marta Alarcón, Diogo Porto, Mercè Amat
Design and construction years 2017-2021
Client Proyecto Calle Llacuna 6 SL
Structure engineer Ofici: Arquitectura / Best Costales-Jaen
MEP engineer PGI
Surveyor Malgosa-Delgado
Photographs José Hevia, Maxime Delvaux

Acne Studios, New York

Location New York, USA
Design Arquitectura-G (Jonathan Arnabat, Jordi Ayala-Bril, Aitor Fuentes and Igor Urdampilleta)
Project team Diogo Porto, Julia Tarnawski, Guillem Bigas
Design and construction years 2020-2021
Client Acne Studios
MEP engineer M-Engineering New York
Lighting Benoit Lalloz
Photographs Maxime Delvaux

Praga Residential Building

Location Barcelona, Spain
Design Arquitectura-G (Jonathan Arnabat, Jordi Ayala-Bril, Aitor Fuentes and Igor Urdampilleta)
Project team Diogo Porto, Mercè Amat
Design and construction years 2019-2021
Client Trend Reformas Group SL
Structure engineer Ofici:Arquitectura
MEP engineer TDI Enginyers
Technical architects Malgosa-Delgado
Photographs Mikael Olsson

Verdi House

Location Barcelona, Spain
Design Arquitectura-G (Jonathan Arnabat, Jordi Ayala-Bril, Aitor Fuentes and Igor Urdampilleta)
Project team Albert Estruga
Design and construction years 2018-2021
Structure engineer Ofici:Arquitectura
MEP engineer TDI Enginyers
Surveyors Malgosa-Delgado
Photographs Maxime Delvaux

Costa House

Location Barcelona, Spain
Design Arquitectura-G (Jonathan Arnabat, Jordi Ayala-Bril, Aitor Fuentes and Igor Urdampilleta)
Project team Albert Estruga, Elena Tarilonte
Design and construction years 2018-2021
Structure engineer Ofici:Arquitectura
MEP engineer TDI Enginyers
Surveyors Malgosa-Delgado
Photographs Maxime Delvaux

Acne Studios, Paris

Location Paris, France
Design Arquitectura-G (Jonathan Arnabat, Jordi Ayala-Bril, Aitor Fuentes and Igor Urdampilleta)
Project team Diogo Porto, Siddartha Rodrigo
Design and construction years 2021-2022
Client Acne Studios
Lighting Benoit Lalloz
Furniture Max Lamb
Photographs Maxime Delvaux

Quinta da Ponte

Location Sintra, Portugal
Design Arquitectura-G (Jonathan Arnabat, Jordi Ayala-Bril, Aitor Fuentes and Igor Urdampilleta)
Project team João Salsa
Design and construction years 2019-
Landscape Architects Global arquitectura paisagista
Structure engineer Gepectrofa
MEP engineer GPIC / Gepectrofa / GET / Amplitude acoustics
Surveyor Nuno Matos

Patio House

Location Aiguablava (Girona), Spain
Design Arquitectura-G (Jonathan Arnabat, Jordi Ayala-Bril, Aitor Fuentes and Igor Urdampilleta)
Project team Diogo Porto, Siddartha Rodrigo, Jesús Jiménez
Design and construction years 2021-
Structure engineer Ofici:Arquitectura
MEP engineer TDI Enginyers
Surveyor Xavier de Bolòs

House in Collserola

Location Barcelona, Spain
Design Arquitectura-G (Jonathan Arnabat, Jordi Ayala-Bril, Aitor Fuentes and Igor Urdampilleta)
Project team Enric Bultó
Design and construction years 2022-

Apartamento Headquarters, Barcelona

Location Barcelona, Spain
Design Arquitectura-G (Jonathan Arnabat, Jordi Ayala-Bril, Aitor Fuentes and Igor Urdampilleta)
Project team Albert Estruga, Albert Guerra, Marta Alarcón, Jesús Jiménez
Design and construction years 2021-
Client Apartamento Publishing SL
Structure engineer Ofici:Arquitectura
MEP engineer TDI Enginyers